1 Introduction

In contrast to the traditional efficient-market hypothesis prediction that market returns are unpredictable, current asset pricing research accepts that equity market returns are largely predictable over long horizons. A number of recent studies have additionally argued that the variance risk premium – the difference between option-implied and realized variance – yields superior forecasts for stock market returns over shorter, within-year horizons (typically one quarter ahead). Examples of these studies include, among others, Bollerslev, Tauchen, and Zhou (2009); Drechsler and Yaron (2011); and Kelly and Jiang (2014). Bollerslev, Tauchen, and Zhou (2009) (henceforth, BTZ) show that the variance risk premium explains a nontrivial fraction of the time-series variation in aggregate stock market returns, and that high (low) variance risk premia predict high (low) future returns.

Drawing on the intuition that investors like good uncertainty – as it increases the potential of substantial gains – but dislike bad uncertainty – as it increases the likelihood of severe losses – we propose a new decomposition of the variance risk premium (VRP), expressed in terms of upside and downside variance risk premia (VRP^U and VRP^D).[1] We show that this decomposition a) identifies the main sources of return predictability uncovered by BTZ and b) characterizes the role of the skewness risk premium (SRP) – measured through the difference between VRP^U and VRP^D – in predicting aggregate stock market returns. We find that on average, and similar to results in Kozhan, Neuberger, and Schneider (2014), over 80% of the VRP is compensation for bearing changes in downside risk. In addition, we show that a) the VRP^D explains the empirical regularities reported by BTZ (including the hump-shaped R^2 and slope parameter patterns), b) the VRP^U's contribution to the results reported by BTZ is at best marginal, and c) there is a contribution of the SRP to the predictability of returns which takes effect beyond the one-quarter-ahead window documented by BTZ.

---

[1] We define the down(up)side variance as the realized variance of the stock market returns for negative (positive) returns, respectively. The down(up)side variance risk premium is the difference between option-implied and realized down(up)side variance. Decomposing variance in this way is pioneered by Barndorff-Nielsen, Kinnebrock, and Shephard (2010), and successfully used in empirical studies by Feunou, Jahan-Parvar, and Tédongap (2013, 2014), among others. In addition, we define the difference between upside and downside variances as the relative upside variance. Feunou, Jahan-Parvar, and Tédongap (2014) show that relative upside variance is a measure of skewness. Based on their work, we use the difference between option-implied and realized relative upside variances as a measure of skewness risk premium.

We show that the prediction power of VRP^D and SRP increases over the term structure of equity returns. In addition, through extensive robustness testing, we show that this result is robust to the inclusion of a wide variety of common pricing factors. This leads to the conclusion that the in-sample predictability of aggregate returns by downside risk and skewness measures introduced here is independent from other common pricing ratios such as the price-dividend ratio, price-earning ratio, or default spread. Based on revealed the in-sample predictive power of these measures, we conduct out-of-sample forecast ability comparisons, and show that in comparison with VRP^D and SRP, other common predictors do not have a superior forecast ability. Finally, we study the link between changes in downside variance risk and skewness risk premia and events or news related to policy uncertainty, comparable to Amengual and Xiu (2014).

Theoretically, we support our findings by a simple endowment equilibrium asset pricing model, where the representative agent is endowed with Epstein and Zin (1989) preferences, and where the consumption growth process is affected by distinct upside and downside shocks. Our model shares some features with Bansal and Yaron (2004), Bollerslev, Tauchen, and Zhou (2009), Segal, Shaliastovich, and Yaron (2015), among others. We show that under common distributional assumptions for shocks to the economy, we can derive the equity risk premium, upside and downside variance risk premium, and skewness risk premium in closed form. Our findings support the empirical findings presented in the paper.

Similar to Colacito, Ghysels, and Meng (2014), our study is not an alternative to jump-tail risk concerns – as studied in Bollerslev and Todorov (2011a,b) – or rare disaster models, in Nakamura, Steinsson, Barro, and Ursúa (2013). Our framework addresses asymmetries that are observed in "normal times". However, our model is well-suited and capable of addressing regularities that emerge from a rare disaster happening, such as the Great Recession of 2007-2009. Essentially, our approach provides simple yet insightful economic intuitions supporting the joint directional and volatility jump risk of Bandi and Renò (2014). We show that our methodology is intuitive, easy to implement, and generates robust predictions that close the horizon gap between short term models such as BTZ and long-horizon predictive models such as Fama and French (1988), Campbell and Shiller (1988), Cochrane (1991), and Lettau and Ludvigson (2001).

Our study is comprised of two natural and linked components. First, we study the role of the VRP^D as the main driver of the within-year predictability results documented by BTZ. In this effort, we highlight the inherent asymmetry in responses of market participants to negative and positive market outcomes. To accomplish this goal, we draw on the vast existing literature on realized and risk-neutral volatility measures and their properties, to construct nonparametric measures of up and downside realized and risk-neutral semi-variances. We then proceed to show empirically how the stylized facts documented in the VRP literature are driven almost entirely by the contribution of VRP^D – the difference between realized and risk-neutral semi-variances extracted from high frequency data. As in Chang, Christoffersen, and Jacobs (2013), our approach avoids the traditional trade-off problem with estimates of higher moments from historical returns data needing long windows to increase precision but short windows to obtain conditional instead of unconditional estimates. Second, we show that using the relative upside variance of Feunou, Jahan-Parvar, and Tédongap (2013, 2014), a nonparametric measure of skewness, we can enhance the predictive power of the variance risk premium to horizons beyond one quarter ahead.[2] Additionally, we find and document the predictive power of a priced factor – the SRP – that fills the gap between the variance risk premium and common long-term equity returns predictors.

Thus, we need reliable measures for realized and risk-neutral variance and skewness. A sizable portion of empirical finance and financial econometrics literature is devoted to measures of volatility. Canonical papers focused on properties and construction of realized volatility are Andersen, Bollerslev, Diebold, and Ebens (2001a); Andersen, Bollerslev, Diebold, and Labys (2003); and Andersen, Bollerslev, Diebold, and Labys (2001b), among others. The construction of realized downside and upside volatilities (also known as realized semi-variances) is addressed in Barndorff-Nielsen, Kinnebrock, and Shephard (2010). We follow the consensus in the literature about construction of these measures. Similarly, based on pioneering studies such as Carr and Madan (1998, 1999, 2001) and Bakshi, Kapadia, and Madan (2003), we have a clear view on how to construct risk-neutral measures of volatility. The construction of option-implied downside and upside volatilities is addressed in Andersen, Bondarenko, and Gonzalez-Perez (2014). Again, we follow the existing literature in this respect.

On the other hand, traditional measures of skewness have well-documented empirical problems.

---

[2]The relative upside variance is the difference between the upside and downside variances.

Kim and White (2004) demonstrate the limitations of estimating the traditional third moment. Harvey and Siddique (1999, 2000) explore time variation in conditional skewness by imposing autoregressive structures. More recently, Feunou, Jahan-Parvar, and Tédongap (2013) and Ghysels, Plazzi, and Valkanov (2011) use Pearson and Bowley's skewness measures, respectively. They overcome many problems associated with the centered third moment, such as the excessive sensitivity to outliers documented in Kim and White (2004), by using alternative and more robust measures.

Neuberger (2012) and Feunou, Jahan-Parvar, and Tédongap (2014) study the properties of realized measures of skewness used in Amaya, Christoffersen, Jacobs, and Vasquez (2013) and Chang, Christoffersen, and Jacobs (2013) in predicting the cross-section of returns at weekly frequency. Building on results presented in Feunou, Jahan-Parvar, and Tédongap (2014, 2013), we first confirm that skewness – measured as the difference between upside and downside variances – is a priced factor. We then provide new evidences that the SRP – measured as the difference between the risk neutral and historical expectations of skewness – is both priced and has superior predictive power.

Our study is also related to the recent macro-finance literature which emphasizes the importance of higher-order risk attitudes such as prudence – a precautionary behavior which characterizes the aversion towards downside risk – in the determination of equilibrium asset prices. Among those studies, Eeckhoudt and Schlesinger (2008) investigate necessary and sufficient conditions for an increase in savings induced by changes in higher-order risk attitudes while Dionne, Li, and Okou (2014) restate a standard consumption-based capital asset pricing model (using the concept of expectation dependence) to show that consumption second-degree expectation dependence risk – a proxy for downside risk which accounts for nearly 80% of the equity premium – is a fundamental source of the macroeconomic risk driving asset prices.

Based on the work of Amengual and Xiu (2014), we document the links that macroeconomic announcements and events share with the SRP and VRP^D. Following Ludvigson and Ng (2009) and Feunou, Fontaine, Taamouti, and Tédongap (2014), we survey in a robustness study the correlations between VRP components and 124 macroeconomic and financial indicators. We find a much lower correlation of the said macroeconomic and financial indicators with VRP^D, as well as with the SRP; the correlation is greater with the VRP, as well as with the VRP^U.

We show through careful robustness exercises that the prediction power of VRP^D and SRP are independent from other common pricing variables. Additionally, in order to address data-mining concerns raised by Goyal and Welch (2008), we conduct out-of-sample forecasting exercises to establish that our predictive variables perform at least as well as other common pricing variables in forecasting excess returns.

The rest of the paper proceeds as follows. In Section 2 we present our decomposition of the VRP and the method for construction of risk-neutral and realized semi-variances, as well as the relative upside variance – which is our measure of skewness. Section 3 details the data used in this study and the empirical construction of predictive variables used in our analysis. We present and discuss our main empirical results in Section 4. Specifically, we intuitively describe the components of variance risk and skewness risk premia, link them to macroeconomic factors, to policy news, discuss their predictive ability, and explore their robustness in Sections 4.1, 4.2, 4.3, 4.4, and 4.5, respectively. In Sections 4.6 and 4.7, we investigate the out-of-sample forecasting performance of our measures. In Section 5, we present a simple equilibrium consumption-based asset pricing model that supports our empirical results. Section 6 concludes.

2 Decomposition of the Variance Risk Premium

In what follows, we decompose equity price changes into positive and negative returns with respect to a suitably chosen threshold. In this study, we set this threshold to zero, but it can assume other values, given the questions to be answered. We sequentially build measures for upside and downside variances, and for skewness. When taken to data, these measures are constructed non-parametrically.

We posit that stock prices or equity market indices such as the S&P 500, S, are defined over the physical probability space characterized by $(\Omega, \mathbb{P}, \mathcal{F})$, where $\{\mathcal{F}_t\}_{t=0}^{\infty} \in \mathcal{F}$ are progressive filters on $\mathcal{F}$. The risk neutral probability measure $\mathbb{Q}$ is related to the physical measure $\mathbb{P}$ through Girsanov's change of measure relation $\frac{d\mathbb{Q}}{d\mathbb{P}}|_{\mathcal{F}_T} = Z_T, T < \infty$. At time t, we denote total equity returns as $R_t^e = (S_t + D_t - S_{t-1})/S_{t-1}$ where D_t is the dividend paid out in period $[t-1, t]$. In high enough sampling frequencies, D_t is effectively equal to zero. Then, we denote the log of prices by $s_t = \ln S_t$, log-returns by $r_t = s_t - s_{t-1}$ and excess log-returns by $r_t^e = r_t - r_t^f$, where r_t^f is the risk-free rate observed at time $t-1$. We obtain cumulative excess returns by summing one-period excess returns,

5

$r_{t \to t+k}^e = \sum_{j=0}^k r_{t+j}^e$, where k is our prediction/forecast horizon.

2.1   Construction of the variance risk premium

We build the variance risk premium following the steps in BTZ as the difference between option-implied and realized variances. Alternatively, these two components could be viewed as variances under risk-neutral and physical measures, respectively. In our approach, this construction requires four distinct steps: building the upside and downside variances under the physical measure, and then doing the same under the risk neutral measure.

For a given trading day t, following Andersen et al. (2003, 2001a), we construct the realized variance of returns as $RV_t = \sum_{j=1}^{n_t} r_{j,t}^2$, where $r_{j,t}^2$ is the jth intraday log-return and n_t is the number of intraday returns observed on that day. We add the squared overnight log-return (the difference in log price between when the market opens at t and when it closes at $t-1$), and we scale the RV_t series to ensure that the sample average realized variance equals the sample variance of daily log-returns. For a give threshold κ, we decompose the realized variance into upside and downside realized variances following Barndorff-Nielsen, Kinnebrock, and Shephard (2010):

$$RV_t^U(\kappa) = \sum_{j=1}^{n_t} r_{j,t}^2 \mathbb{I}_{[r_{j,t} > \kappa]}, \tag{1}$$

$$RV_t^D(\kappa) = \sum_{j=1}^{n_t} r_{j,t}^2 \mathbb{I}_{[r_{j,t} \leq \kappa]}. \tag{2}$$

We add the squared overnight "positive" log-return (exceeding the threshold κ) to the upside realized variance RV_t^U, and the squared overnight "negative" log-return (falling below the threshold κ) to the downside realized variance RV_t^D. Because the daily realized variance sums the upside and the downside realized variances, we apply the same scale to the two components of the realized variance. Specifically, we multiply both components by the ratio of the sample variance of daily log-returns over the sample average of the (pre-scaled) realized variance.

For a given horizon h, we obtain the cumulative realized quantities by summing the one-day realized quantities over the h periods:

$$RV_{t,h}^U(\kappa) = \sum_{j=1}^{h} RV_{t+j}^U(\kappa),$$

$$RV_{t,h}^D(\kappa) = \sum_{j=1}^{h} RV_{t+j}^D(\kappa),$$

$$RV_{t,h} = \sum_{j=1}^{h} RV_{t+j}(\kappa). \tag{3}$$

By construction, the cumulative realized variance adds up the cumulative realized upside and downside variances:

$$RV_{t,h} \equiv RV_{t,h}^U(\kappa) + RV_{t,h}^D(\kappa). \tag{4}$$

Next, we characterize the VRP of BTZ through premia accrued to bearing upside and downside variance risks, following these steps:

$$
\begin{aligned}
VRP_{t,h} &= \mathbb{E}_t^{\mathbb{Q}}[RV_{t,h}] - \mathbb{E}_t^{\mathbb{P}}[RV_{t,h}], \\
&= \left(\mathbb{E}_t^{\mathbb{Q}}[RV_{t,h}^U(\kappa)] - \mathbb{E}_t^{\mathbb{P}}[RV_{t,h}^U(\kappa)] \right) + \left(\mathbb{E}_t^{\mathbb{Q}}[RV_{t,h}^D(\kappa)] - \mathbb{E}_t^{\mathbb{P}}[RV_{t,h}^D(\kappa)] \right), \\
VRP_{t,h} &\equiv VRP_{t,h}^U(\kappa) + VRP_{t,h}^D(\kappa). \tag{5}
\end{aligned}
$$

Eq. (5) represents the decomposition of the VRP of BTZ into upside and downside variance risk premia – $VRP_{t,h}^U(\kappa)$ and $VRP_{t,h}^D(\kappa)$, respectively – that lies at the heart of our analysis.

2.1.1 Construction of P-expectation

The goal here is to evaluate $\mathbb{E}_t^{\mathbb{P}}[RV_{t,h}^U(\kappa)]$ and $\mathbb{E}_t^{\mathbb{P}}[RV_{t,h}^D(\kappa)]$. To this end, we consider three specifications:

- Random Walk

$$\mathbb{E}_t^{\mathbb{P}}[RV_{t,h}^{U/D}(\kappa)] = RV_{t-h,h}^{U/D}(\kappa),$$

where U/D stands for "U or D"; this is the model used in BTZ.

- U/D-HAR

$$\mathbb{E}_t^{\mathbb{P}}[RV_{t+1}^{U/D}(\kappa)] = \omega^{U/D} + \beta_d^{U/D}RV_t^{U/D}(\kappa) + \beta_w^{U/D}RV_{t,5}^{U/D}(\kappa) + \beta_m^{U/D}RV_{t,20}^{U/D}(\kappa).$$

- M-HAR

$$\mathbb{E}_t^{\mathbb{P}}[MRV_{t+1}(\kappa)] = \omega + \beta_d MRV_t(\kappa) + \beta_w MRV_{t,5}(\kappa) + \beta_m MRV_{t,20}(\kappa),$$

where $MRV_{t,h}(\kappa) \equiv (RV_{t,h}^{U}(\kappa), RV_{t,h}^{D}(\kappa))'$.

Both U/D-HAR and M-HAR specifications mimic Corsi (2009)'s HAR-RV model. To get genuine expected values for realized measures that are not contaminated by forward bias or use of contemporaneous data, we perform an out-of-sample forecasting exercise to predict the three realized variances, at different horizons, corresponding to 1, 2, 3, 6, 9, 12, 18 and 24 months ahead. In our subsequent analysis, we find that these alternative specifications provide similar results. Hence, for simplicity and to save space, we only report the results based on the random walk model.

2.1.2 Construction of Q-expectation

To build the risk-neutral expectation of $RV_{t,h}$, we follow the methodology of Andersen and Bondarenko (2007):

$$
\begin{aligned}
\mathbb{E}_t^{\mathbb{Q}}[RV_{t,h}^{U}(\kappa)] &\approx \mathbb{E}_t^{\mathbb{Q}}\Big[\int_t^{t+h} \sigma_u^2 \mathbb{I}_{[\ln(F_u|F_t)>\kappa]}du\Big], \\
&= \mathbb{E}_t^{\mathbb{Q}}\Big[\int_t^{t+h} \sigma_u^2 \mathbb{I}_{[F_u>F_t\exp(\kappa)]}du\Big].
\end{aligned}
$$

Thus,

$$
\begin{aligned}
\mathbb{E}_t^{\mathbb{Q}}[RV_{t,h}^{U}(\kappa)] &\approx 2\int_{F_t\exp(\kappa)}^{\infty} \frac{M_0(\underline{S})}{\underline{S}^2}d\underline{S}, \\
M_0(\underline{S}) &= \min(P_t(\underline{S}), C_t(\underline{S})),
\end{aligned}
\tag{6}
$$

where, $P_t(\underline{S}), C_t(\underline{S})$, and $\underline{S}$ are prices of European put and call options (with maturity h), and the strike price of the underlying asset, respectively. F_t is the price of a future contract at time t, defined as $F_t = S_t \exp(r_t^f h)$. Similarly for $\mathbb{E}_t^{\mathbb{Q}}[RV_{t,h}^D(\kappa)]$, we get:

$$\mathbb{E}_t^{\mathbb{Q}}[RV_{t,h}^D(\kappa)] \approx 2 \int_{-\infty}^{F_t \exp(\kappa)} \frac{M_0(\underline{S})}{\underline{S}^2} d\underline{S}. \tag{7}$$

We simplify our notation by renaming $\mathbb{E}_t^{\mathbb{Q}}[RV_{t,h}^U(\kappa)]$ and $\mathbb{E}_t^{\mathbb{Q}}[RV_{t,h}^D(\kappa)]$ as

$$IV_{t,h}^U = \mathbb{E}_t^{\mathbb{Q}}[RV_{t,h}^U(\kappa)], \tag{8}$$

$$IV_{t,h}^D = \mathbb{E}_t^{\mathbb{Q}}[RV_{t,h}^D(\kappa)]. \tag{9}$$

We refer to $IV_{t,h}^{U/D}$ as the "risk-neutral semi-variance" or "implied semi-variance" of returns. These quantities are conditioned on the threshold value κ, which we suppress to simplify notation. As evident in this section, our measures of realized and implied volatility are model-free.

2.2 Construction of the skewness risk premium

Proposition 2.1 in Feunou, Jahan-Parvar, and Tédongap (2014) shows that the difference between upside and downside variances (standardized by total variance) meets the criteria set forth by Groeneveld and Meeden (1984) as a measure for skewness. It is invariant to affine transformation of a random variable, is an odd function of a random variable, and assumes zero value for a symmetrically distributed random variable. Since this skewness measure only depends on the existence of the second moment, it can be computed in instances when the third moment of a distribution is undefined; see Feunou, Jahan-Parvar, and Tédongap (2014).

To build this measure of skewness, denoted as $RSV_{t,h}$, we simply subtract downside variance from upside semi-variance:

$$RSV_{t,h}(\kappa) = RV_{t,h}^U(\kappa) - RV_{t,h}^D(\kappa). \tag{10}$$

Thus, if $RSV_{t,h}(\kappa) < 0$ we have a left-skewed distribution, and when $RSV_{t,h}(\kappa) > 0$ it is right-skewed.

In addition, we introduce the notion of a skewness risk premium, closely resembling the variance risk premium. It can be shown that the skewness risk premium is the difference between the two components of the VRP and is defined as the difference between risk neutral and objective expectations of the realized skewness. We denote skewness risk premium by $SRP_{t,h}$, and construct it as follows:

$$SRP_{t,h} = \mathbb{E}^{\mathbb{Q}}[RSV_{t,h}] - \mathbb{E}^{\mathbb{P}}[RSV_{t,h}],$$
$$SRP_{t,h} = VRP_{t,h}^{U}(\kappa) - VRP_{t,h}^{D}(\kappa). \tag{11}$$

If $RSV_{t,h} < 0$, we view $SRP_{t,h}$ as a skewness premium – the compensation for an agent who bears downside risk. On the other hand, if $RSV_{t,h} > 0$, we view $SRP_{t,h}$ as a skewness discount – the amount that the agent is willing to pay to secure a positive return on an investment.

Since this measure of skewness risk premium is nonparametric and model-free, it is easier to implement and interpret than competing parametric counterparts. Also, as mentioned earlier, through a suitable choice of κ it can be used to investigate tail behavior of returns – if such an exercise is desired. In this study, we are not interested in this application.

3 Data

BTZ results establish that the difference between current returns variation (approximated by RV) and the markets risk-neutral expectation of future returns variation (approximated by IV) is a useful predictor of the future returns; it deos this by effectively isolating the systematic risk associated with the volatility-of-volatility. In this study, we adapt BTZ's methodology and use modified measures introduced in Section 2.1. As shown above, these measures also lead to construction of SRP as a byproduct. We thus need suitable data to construct excess returns, realized semi-variances ($RV^{U/D}$), and risk-neutral semi-variances ($IV^{U/D}$). In what follows, we discuss the raw data and methods we use to construct our empirical measures. Throughout the study, we set $\kappa = 0$.

3.1 Excess returns

Following BTZ, we are interested in documenting the prediction power of upside and downside variances risk premia, as well as the skewness risk premium for monthly excess returns of an equity market portfolio. Our empirical analysis is based on the S&P 500 composite index as a proxy for the aggregate market portfolio. Since our study requires reliable high-frequency data and option-implied volatilities, our sample spans the September 1996 to December 2010 period. We construct the excess returns by subtracting 3-month Treasury Bill rates from log-differences in the S&P 500 composite index, sampled at the end of each month.

We report the summary statistics of equity returns in Panel A of Table 1. We report annualized mean, median, and standard deviations of returns in percentages. The table also reports monthly skewness, excess kurtosis, and the first order autoregressive coefficient ($AR(1)$) for the S&P 500 monthly excess returns.

3.2 Options data and risk-neutral variances

Since our study hinges on decomposition of the variance process into upside and downside semi-variances, we cannot follow BTZ by using VIX as a measure of risk-neutral volatility. As a result, we construct our own measures of risk-neutral upside and downside variances ($IV^{U/D}$). We use two sources of data to construct upside and downside IV measures. First, we obtain from OptionMetrics Ivy DB daily data of European-style put and call options on the S&P 500 index. We then match these option data with return series on the underlying S&P 500 index and risk-free rates downloaded from CRSP files.

For each day in the sample period, which begins in September 1996 and ends in December 2010, we sort call and put option data by maturity and strike price. We construct option prices by averaging the bid and ask quotes for each contract. To obtain consistent risk-neutral moments, we preprocess the data by applying the same filters as in Chang, Christoffersen, and Jacobs (2013).[3] We only consider out-of-the-money (OTM) contracts. Such contracts are the most traded, and thus, the most liquid options. Thus, we discard call options with moneyness levels – the ratios of strike prices to the underlying asset price – lower than 97% ($\underline{S}/S < 0.97$). Similarly, we discard put options with moneyness levels greater than 103% ($\underline{S}/S > 1.03$). Raw option data contain discontinuous strike prices. Therefore, on each day and for any given maturity, we interpolate implied volatilities over a finely-discretized moneyness domain ($\underline{S}/S$), using a cubic spline to obtain a dense set of implied volatilities. We restrict the interpolation procedure to days that have at least two OTM

---

[3]That is, we discard options with zero bids, those with average quotes less than $3/8, and those whose quotes violate common no-arbitrage restrictions.

call prices and two OTM put prices available.

For out-of-range moneyness levels (below or above the observed moneyness levels in the market), we extrapolate the implied volatility of the lowest or highest available strike price. We perform this interpolation-extrapolation procedure to obtain a fine grid of 1000 implied volatilities, for moneyness levels between 0.01 % and 300%. We then map these implied volatilities into call and put prices. Call prices are constructed for moneyness levels larger than 100% ($\underline{S}/S > 1$) whereas put prices are generated from moneyness levels smaller than 100% ($\underline{S}/S < 1$). We approximate the integrals using a recursive adaptive Lobatto quadrature. Finally, for any given future horizon of interest (1 to 24 months), we employ a linear interpolation to compute the corresponding moments, and rely on Eq. (6) and (7) to compute the upside and downside risk-neutral variance measures. We obtain 3,860 daily observations of upside/downside risk-neutral variances for maturities from 1 to 24 months.

An important issue in the construction of risk-neutral measures is the respective density of put and call contracts, especially for deep OTM contracts. Explicitly, precise computation of risk-neutral volatility components hinges on comparable numbers of OTM put and call contracts in longer horizon maturities (18 to 24 months). Our data set provides a rich environment which supports this data construction exercise. As clear from Table 2, while there are more OTM put contracts than OTM call contracts by any of the three measures used – moneyness, maturity, or VIX level – the respective numbers of contracts are comparable. In addition, Figure 1 shows that the growth of these contracts has continued unabated. We conclude that our construction of risk-neutral volatility components is not subject to bias due to sparsity of data in deep OTM contracts.

Our computations are based on decompiling the variance risk premium based on realized returns to be above or below a cut-off point, $\kappa = 0$. However, κ is not directly applicable to the risk-neutral probability space. Thus, we make the appropriate transformation to use our cut-off point by letting r^f represent the instantaneous risk-free rate, and denote time-to-maturity by τ. Then, for the market price index at time t, we define the applicable cut-off point $B = F_t \exp(\kappa)$ using the forward price $F_t = S_t \exp(r^f \tau)$. We then use B to compute the risk-neutral upside and downside variances, which thus can be viewed as a model-free *corridor* risk-neutral volatilities as discussed in Andersen, Bondarenko, and Gonzalez-Perez (2014); Andersen and Bondarenko (2007) and Carr and Madan (1999), among others.

Panel B of Table 1 reports the summary statistics of risk-neutral volatility measures. As expected, these series are persistent – $AR(1)$ parameters are all above 0.95 – and demonstrate significant skewness and excess kurtosis. It is also clear that the main factor behind volatility behavior is the downside variance.

Figure 2 provides a stark demonstration of this point. It is immediately obvious that the contribution of upside variance to risk-neutral volatility is considerably less than that of downside variance. In fact, for most maturities, the median upside variance is about 50 to 80% smaller than the median downside variance. As time-to-maturity increases – a good measure for future expectations – the size of the median IV^U decreases. Notice that the size of this quantity is never as large as the median IV^D. On the other hand, the size of median IV^D increases uniformly over time-to-maturity, is close to median risk-neutral volatility values at each corresponding point in time-to-maturity, and demonstrates the same pattern of median risk-neutral volatility.

Thus, compared to its upside counterpart, the downside risk-neutral variance is clearly the main component of the risk-neutral volatility. We buttress this claim in the remainder of the paper through empirical analysis.

3.3 High frequency data and realized variance components

We use daily close-to-close S&P 500 returns, realized variances data computed from 5-minute intraday S&P 500 prices and 3-Month Treasury Bill Rates for the period September 1996 to December 2010, which yields a total of 3,608 daily observations. The data is available through the Institute of Financial Markets.

To construct the daily $RV^{U/D}$s series, we use intraday S&P 500 data. We sum the 5-minute squared negative returns for the downside realized variance (RV^D) and the 5-minute squared positive returns for the upside realized variance (RV^U). We nest add the daily squared overnight negative returns to the downside semi-variance, and daily squared overnight positive returns to the upside realized variance. The overnight returns are computed for 4:00 PM to 9:30 AM. The total realized variance is obtained by adding the downside and the upside realized variance. For the three series, we use a multiplicative scaling of the average total realized variance series to match the unconditional variance of S&P 500 returns.[4]

4 Empirical Results

In this section, we provide economic intuition and empirical support for our proposed decomposition of the variance risk premium. First, based on a sound financial rationale, we intuitively describe the expected behavior of the components of variance risk premium and skewness risk premium. We also present some empirical facts about the size and variability of these components. Since our approach is non-parametric, these facts stand as challenges for realistic models (reduced-form and general equilibrium). Second, we establish that decomposing the variance risk premium into upside and downside variance risk premia reveals that while VRP components are positively correlated with several macroeconomic and financial indicators, the level of spanning across these components differ. Third, we study the reaction of variance risk premium components to macroeconomic and financial announcements. In particular, we are interested in uncovering the relationship between announcements that reduce or resolve uncertainty surrounding monetary or fiscal policy. Fourth, we provide an extensive investigation of predictability of equity premia, based on variance premium and its components as well as skewness risk premium. We empirically demonstrate the contribution of downside risk and skewness risk premia and characterize the sources of VRP predictability documented by BTZ. Subsequently, we provide comprehensive robustness study. Finally, we conclude with out-of-sample forecast ability properties of our proposed predictors – downside variance risk and skewness risk premia.

4.1 Description of the variance risk premium components

The VRP can be interpreted as the premium a market participant is willing to pay to hedge against variation in future realized volatilities. It is expected to be positive because of the intuition that risk-averse investors dislike large swings in volatility, especially in "bad times". This intuition is rationalized within the general equilibrium model of BTZ, where it is shown that the variance risk premium is in general positive and proportional to the volatility of volatility. We confirm these

---

[4]Hansen and Lunde (2006) discuss various approaches to adjusting open-to-close RVs.

findings by reporting in Table 1 some summary statistics. We also plot the time-series of VRP, its components, and SRP in Figure 7. From 1996 to 2010, we can see that the variance risk premium is positive most of the time, and remains high in uncertain times.

However, several studies including Feunou, Jahan-Parvar, and Tédongap (2013) and Segal, Shaliastovich, and Yaron (2015) show that there are good and bad uncertainties. On one hand, market participants like good uncertainty when returns are positive, as it signals the potential of earning an even higher return. In other words, risk-averse agents like upside variations, and are willing to pay to be exposed to fluctuations in the upside variance. This argument should induce a negative expected value for VRP^U. Table 1 clearly illustrates these intuitions as the average VRP^U is about -4.41%. Moreover, Figure 7 shows that VRP^U is usually negative through our sample period. On the other hand, investors dislike bad uncertainty (when returns are negative), as it increases the likelihood of losses. Because risk averse agents dislike downside variations, they are willing to pay a premium to hedge against fluctuations in future downside variances. Therefore, VRP^D is expected to be positive most of the time. These intuitions are supported by the empirical evidence in Table 1, where the average downside variance premium is about 3.4%, and in Figure 7, where we observe that VRP^D is usually positive.

Upside and downside variance risk premia tend to have opposite signs. Thus, the (total) variance risk premium that sums these two components essentially mixes together market participants' (asymmetric) views about good and bad uncertainties. This entails that positive (total) variance risk premium reflects the fact that investors are willing to pay more in order to hedge against changes in bad uncertainty than that for exposure to variations in good uncertainty.

Hence, focusing on the (total) variance risk premium does not provide a detailed overview of the trade-off between good and bad uncertainties, as a small positive number does not necessarily imply a lower level of risk and/or risk aversion. It is rather an indication of a smaller difference between what agents are willing to pay for downside variation hedging versus upside variation exposure.

Building on the same intuition, the sign of the SRP stems from the expected behavior of the two components of the VRP. The SRP is obtained by subtracting VRP^D from VRP^U. Given that (on average) VRP^U appears negative whereas VRP^D tends to be positive, the SRP is expected to be negative. This intuition is supported by Figure 7 where the average skewness risk premium is

-7.8%. Alternatively, this negative sign may be interpreted as follows: market participants prefer higher skewness, and would like to be exposed to variations in future skewness.

Table 1 also reveals highly persistent, negatively-skewed, and fat-tailed distributions for (down/upside) variance and skewness risk premia. Nonetheless, upside variance and skewness risk premia appear more left-skewed and leptokurtic as compared to (total) variance and downside variance risk premia.

4.2 Links to macroeconomic and financial indicators

Following Ludvigson and Ng (2009) and Feunou et al. (2014), we survey the correlations of variance, upside variance, downside variance, and skewness risk premia with 124 financial and economic indicators. We carry out this exercise to document the contemporaneous correlation of variance and skewness risk premia with well-known macroeconomic and financial variables. The VRP and its components are predictors of risk in financial markets, that is, an increase in VRP or VRP^D implies expectations of elevated risk levels in the future and hence compensation for bearing that risk. Fama and French (1989) document the counter-cyclical behavior of the equity premium: investors demand a higher equity premium in bad times. It follows that VRP should be mildly pro-cyclical and positively correlated with cyclical macroeconomic and financial variables. The relationship between SRP and macroeconomic and financial factors is an empirically open issue that we address in this study. Finally, we are interested in the spanning of VRP, its components, and SRP by macroeconomic and financial factors. Briefly, low levels of spanning imply the information content in the risk premium measures that is orthogonal to the information content of common financial or economic quantities.

In our empirical investigation, we focus on contemporaneous correlations and adjusted R^2s since, given orthonormal factors, the regression coefficients depend on identification assumptions. The analysis and results here are based on a contemporaneous univariate regression model, where the dependent variable is one of the variance risk premium or skewness measures, and the independent variable is one of the variables studied by Feunou et al. (2014).[5]

Table 3 reports the ten variables that yield the highest R^2s for each (semi-)variance risk premium component and their respective slope parameter Student-t statistics. The composition of the factors

---

[5]The complete list of these variables and supplementary results regarding our analysis are available in an online Appendix.

that explain the variation in variance, upside variance, downside variance, and skewness risk premia and the size of the adjusted R^2s above the 10% threshold wide-ranging. Clearly, variables listed on this table all yield slope parameters statistically different from zero at conventional significance levels, as evidenced by the high Student-t statistics.

Slope parameters for VRP and its components are all positive, and imply positive correlation with the mainly pro-cyclical macroeconomic variables listed in the table. Overall, payroll measures and industrial production indices are the most important predictors for VRP and its components, accounting for virtually all top predictors for these quantities. Total payroll in the private sector is the most powerful contemporaneous predictor for VRP and VRP^U. It yields an adjusted R^2 of over 50% for VRP^U and 40% for VRP. The level of explanatory power of this variable, measured by the adjusted R^2, drops to under 25% for VRP^D.

Slope parameters for the regression model containing SRP as the predicted variable and macroeconomic and financial variables as predictors, imply a negative contemporaneous correlation. The top variables with a significant correlation with SRP differ from those in the other three panels of Table 3. For example, total payroll in the private sector does not have much explanatory power for the SRP; it yields an adjusted R^2 equal to 11.63% and is the 9th variable in the list. The sources of predictability for the SRP – while much weaker – are diverse. Price indices and bond yields have weak, contemporaneous prediction power for the SRP. Since payroll measures and bond yields, especially those with shorter maturities such as 6-month Treasury Bills are pro-cyclical, these findings imply counter-cyclical behavior for the SRP.

Together, the regularities discussed above lead us to conclude that the common financial and macroeconomic indicators do not span well the VRP components or SRP, since none of them explains more than 53% of the variation in these premia contemporaneously. Moreover, these indicators seem to have the least success spanning downside variance and skewness risk premia. This observation sheds further light on the success of these two factors in predicting equity premia – their information content is largely uncorrelated with that of a large set of macroeconomic and financial variables. Similarly, the relatively high correlation of VRP^U with several macroeconomic variables partially explains its poor predictive performance with respect to the equity premium – it contains less unspanned information.

4.3 Reaction to announcements and events

Amengual and Xiu (2014) study the impact on decisions and announcements that reduce or resolve uncertainty, especially regarding monetary and fiscal policies. We use the same set of events compiled by Amengual and Xiu (2014) to study the impact of events, such as FOMC announcements, speeches by Federal Reserve officials and the Presidents of the United States, as well as economic and political news that had significant impact on market returns or measures of market volatility. The events are summarized in Table 4.

We report in Table 5 the changes in the variance, upside variance, downside variance, and skewness risk premia as well as their end-of-the-day levels on event dates. The most striking outcome from this exercise is the observation that across the board and for all variance risk components and skewness risk premia, policy announcements that resolve financial or monetary uncertainty, also reduce the premia. The impact on the SRP, however, is mixed: announcements can increase or decrease the size of this premium. This observation, by construction, hinges on the size of the reduction imputed by the announcement on VRP^U and VRP^D. That said, in 16 out of 22 events studied, the impact of events on the SRP is negative.

In addition to matching the events recorded by Amengual and Xiu (2014) to changes in variance risk premium components, we conducted an exercise to perform targeted searches for the largest changes in variance risk premium components in suitably chosen date intervals that contain the event date – in this case, a trading week before and after the event date – to identify the largest changes in (semi-)variance risk premium components in that interval. The results are not fundamentally different from what is reported in Table 5. Most large movements are very close to the event date. Thus they are not reported to save space, but are available upon request.

We may view these observations as evidence that resolution of policy uncertainty or reduction of political tensions have a negative impact on premia demanded by the market participants to bear variance or skewness risk.

4.4 Predictability of the equity premium

BTZ derive a theoretical model where the VRP emerges as the main driver of time variation in the equity premium. They show both theoretically and empirically that a higher VRP predicts higher future excess returns. Intuitively, the variance risk premium proxies the premium associated with the volatility of volatility, which not only reflects how future random returns vary, but also assesses fluctuations in the tail thickness of the future returns distribution.

Because the VRP sums downside and upside variance risk premia, BTZ's framework entails imposing the same coefficient on both (upside and downside) components of the VRP when they are jointly included in a predictive regression of excess returns. However, such a constraint seems very restrictive given the asymmetric views of investors on good uncertainty – proneness to upward variability – versus bad uncertainty – aversion to downward variability. Sections 4.1, 4.2 and 4.3 document that both VRP^D and VRP^U have intrinsically different features.

Intuitively, risk-averse investors like variability in positive outcomes of returns, but dislike it in negative outcomes. Hence in a joint regression, we expect coefficient of VRP^D to be positive and that of VRP^U to be negative. These observations boil down to a simple intuition: risk-averse investors ask for a premium to face risks they do not like while they are willing to pay for exposure to favorable uncertainties – risks they like. Panel A in Table 9 reports results of joint regressions of excess returns on both VRP^D and VRP^U. Our findings confirm our intuition at all horizons.

It is important to point out that by highlighting the disparities between upside and downside variance risk premia, we do not intend to invalidate BTZ's model. Their study is built to rationalize the importance of variance risk premium in explaining the dynamics of the equity premium. Our study pushes further, by documenting that the SRP is pivotal in disentangling the upside from the downside premium related to future changes in variability. Thus, our goal is to build on BTZ's framework, showing that introducing asymmetry in the VRP analysis provides additional flexibility to the trade-off between return first and second moment risk premia. Ultimately, our approach is intended to strengthen the concept behind the variance risk premium of BTZ.

Our results are based on a simple linear regression of k-step-ahead cumulative S&P 500 excess returns on values of a set of predictors that include the VRP, VRP^U, VRP^D, and SRP. Following the results of Ang and Bekaert (2007), reported Student's t-statistics are based on heteroscedasticity and serial correlation consistent standard errors that explicitly take account of the overlap in the regressions, as advocated by Hodrick (1992). The model used for our analysis is simply:

$$r^e_{t \to t+k} = \beta_0 + \beta_1 x_t(h) + \epsilon_{t \to t+k}, \tag{12}$$

where $r_{t \to t+k}$ is the cumulative excess returns between time t, $t+k$, $x_t(h)$ is one of the predictors discussed in Sections 2.1 and 2.2 at time t, h is the construction horizon of $x_t(h)$, and ϵ_t is a zero-mean error term. We focus our discussion on the significance of the estimated slope coefficients (β_1s), determined by the robust Student-t statistics. We report the predictive ability of regressions, measured by the corresponding adjusted R^2s. For highly persistent predictor variables, the R^2s for the overlapping multi-period return regressions must be interpreted with caution, as noted by BTZ and Jacquier and Okou (2014), among others.

Following our discussion of the observed mildly cyclical behavior of the VRP and those of VRP^U and VRP^D in Section 4.2, and given the counter-cyclical behavior of the equity premium, we expect to observe positive slope parameters in the regression model in equation (12), when $x_t(h)$ is one of variance risk premia quantities.

We decompose the contribution of our predictors to show that: 1) predictability results documented by BTZ are driven by the downside variance risk premium, 2) predictability results are mainly driven by risk-neutral expectations – thus, risk neutral measures contribute more than realized measures, and 3) the contribution of the skewness risk premium increases as a function of both the predictability horizon (k) and construction horizon (h).

Our empirical findings, presented in Tables 6 to 9, support all three claims made above. In Panel A, Table 6, we show that the two main regularities uncovered by BTZ, hump-shaped increase in robust Student-t statistics and adjusted R^2s reaching their maximum at $k = 3$ (one quarter ahead), are present in the data. Both regularities are visible in the upper-left-hand-side plots in Figures 4 and 5. These effects, however, weaken as the construction horizon (h) increases from one month to three months or more: the predictability pattern weakens and then largely disappears for $h > 6$.

Panel B of Table 6 reports the predictability results based on using VRP^D as the predictor. A visual representation of these results is available in the upper-right-hand-side plots in Figures 4 and 5. It is immediately obvious that both regularities observed in the VRP predictive regressions are preserved. We observe the hump-shaped pattern for Student's t-statistics and the adjusted R^2s reaching their maximum between $k = 3$ or $k = 6$ months. Moreover, these results are more robust

20

to the construction horizon of the predictor. We notice that in contrast to the VRP results – where predictability is only present for monthly or quarterly constructed risk premia – the VRP^D results are largely robust to construction horizons; the slope parameters are statistically different from zero even for annually constructed downside variance risk premia ($h = 12$). Moreover, the VRP^D results yield higher adjusted R^2s compared with the VRP regressions at similar prediction horizons, an observation that we interpret as the superior ability of the VRP^D to explain the variation in aggregate excess returns. Last but not least, we notice a gradual shift in prediction results from the familiar one-quarter-ahead peak of predictability documented by BTZ to 9-12-months-ahead peaks, once we increase the construction horizon h. Based on these results, we infer that the the VRP^D is the likely candidate to explain the predictive power of VRP, documented by BTZ.

Our results for predictability based on the VRP^U, reported in Panel C of Table 6 and the two lower left-hand-side plots in Figures 4 and 5, are weak. The hump-shaped pattern in both robust Student's t-statistics and in adjusted R^2s, while present, is significantly weaker than the results reported by BTZ. Once we increase the construction horizon h, these results are lost. We conclude that bearing upside variance risk does not appear to be an important contributor to the equity premium, and hence, is not a good predictor of this quantity. In addition, we interpret these findings as a low contribution of the VRP^U to overall VRP.

We observe a set of interesting regularities, however, when we use the SRP as our predictor. These results are reported in Panel D of Table 6 and the bottom-right-hand-side plots in Figures 4 and 5. It is immediately clear that this factor displays predictive power at longer horizons than the VRP. For monthly excess returns, the SRP slope coefficient is statistically different from zero at prediction horizons of 6-months-ahead or longer. At $k = 6$, the adjusted R^2 of the SRP is comparable in size with that of the VRP (2.30% against 3.65%, respectively) and is strictly greater thereafter. At $k = 6$, the adjusted R^2 for the monthly excess return regression based on the SRP is smaller than that of the VRP^D. However, their sizes are comparable at $k = 9$ and $k = 12$ months ahead. Both trends strengthen as we consider higher aggregation levels for excess returns. At the semi-annual construction level ($h = 6$), the SRP already has more predictive power than both the VRP and VRP^D at a quarter-ahead prediction horizon. The increase in adjusted R^2s of the SRP is not monotonic in the construction horizon level. We can detect a maximum at a roughly three-quarters-ahead prediction window for semi-annual and annually constructed SRPs. This observation implies that this factor is the intermediate link between one-quarter-ahead predictability using the VRP uncovered by BTZ and the long-term predictors such as the price-dividend ratio, dividend yield, or consumption-wealth ratio of Lettau and Ludvigson (2001). We conclude that predictability of cumulative excess returns by the SRP increases in both prediction horizon, k, and construction horizon, h, for the SRP.

At this point, it is natural to inquire about including both VRP components in a predictive regression. We present the empirical evidence from this estimation in Panel A of Table 9. After inclusion of the VRP^U and VRP^D in the same regression, the statistical significance of the VRP^U's slope parameters is broadly lost. We also notice a sign change in Student's t-statistics associated with the estimated slope parameters of the VRP^U and VRP^D. This observation, as documented in Feunou, Jahan-Parvar, and Tédongap (2013), lends credibility to the role of the SRP as a predictor of aggregated excess returns.[6]

We claim that the patterns discussed above, and hence the predictive power of the VRP, VRP^D, and SRP are rooted in expectations. That is, the driving force behind our results, as well as those of BTZ, are expected risk-neutral measures of the volatility components. To show the empirical findings supporting our claim, we run predictive regressions, using Equation (12). Instead of using the "premia" employed so far, we use realized and risk-neutral measures of variances, up- and downside variances, and skewness for x_t, based on our discussions in Section 2, respectively.

Our empirical findings using risk-neutral volatility measures are available in Table 7. In Panel A, we report the results of running a predictive regression when the predictor is the risk-neutral variance obtained from direct application of the Andersen and Bondarenko (2007) method. It is clear that the estimated slope parameters are statistically different from zero for $k \geq 3$ at most construction horizons, h. The reported adjusted R^2s also imply that the predictive regressions have explanatory power for aggregate excess return variations at $k \geq 3$. The same patterns are discernible for risk-neutral downside and upside variances (Panels B and C) and risk-neutral skewness (Panel D). Adjusted R^2s reported are lower than those reported in Table 6, and these measures of variation

---

[6]Briefly, based on arguments similar to those advanced by Feunou, Jahan-Parvar, and Tédongap (2013), we expect estimated parameters of the VRP^U and VRP^D to have opposite signs, and be statistically "close". As such, they imply that the SRP is the factor we should have included.

yield statistically significant slope parameters at longer prediction horizons than what we observe for the VRP and its components. Taken together, these observations imply that using the premium (rather than the risk-neutral variation) yields better predictions.

However, in comparison with realized (physical) variation measures, risk-neutral measures yield better results. The analysis using realized variation measures are available in Table 8. It is obvious that by themselves, the realized measures do not yield reasonable predictability, an observation corroborated by empirical findings of Bekaert, Engstrom, and Ermolov (2014). The majority of estimated slope parameters are statistically indistinguishable from zero, and adjusted R^2s are low. Inclusion of both risk-neutral or realized variance components does not change our findings dramatically, as demonstrated in Panels B and C of Table 9.

We observe in Panel D of Table 8 and in Panel C of 9 statistical significance and notable adjusted R^2s for realized skewness in long prediction horizons ($k \geq 6$) and for construction horizons ($h \geq 6$). By itself (as opposed to the SRP studied earlier), the realized skewness lacks predictive power in low construction or prediction horizons. Based on our results presented in Table 6, we argue that the SRP (and not the realized skewness) is a more suitable predictive factor, as it overcomes these two shortcomings.

A visual representation of the prediction power of risk neutral (integrated) and physical (realized) variation components is available in Figure 6. Given the weak performance of realized measures, it is easy to conclude that realized variation plays a secondary role to risk-neutral variation measures in driving the predictability results documented by BTZ or in this study. However, we need both elements in construction of the variance or skewness risk premia since realized or risk-neutral measures individually posses inferior prediction power.

4.5 Robustness

We perform extensive robustness exercises to document the prediction power of the VRP^D and SRP for aggregate excess returns, in the presence of traditional predictor variables. The goal is to highlight the contribution of our proposed variables in a wider empirical context. Simply put, we observe that predictive power does not disappear when we include other pricing variables, implying that the VRP^D and SRP are not simply proxies for other well-known pricing ratios.

Following BTZ and Feunou et al. (2014) among many others, we include equity pricing measures such as log price-dividend ratio ($\log(p_t/d_t)$), lagged log price-dividend ratio ($\log(p_{t-1}/d_t)$, and log price-earning ratio ($\log(p_t/e_t)$); yield and spread measures such as term spread (tms_t) – the difference between 10-year U.S. Treasury Bond yield and 3-month U.S. Treasury Bill yield –, default spread (dfs_t) – the difference between BBB and AAA corporate bond yields –; CPI inflation ($infl_t$), and finally Kelly and Pruitt (2013) partial least squares-based, cross-sectional in-sample and out-of-sample predictive factors ($kpis_t$ and $kpos_t$, respectively).

We consider two periods for our analysis: our full sample – September 1996 to December 2010 – and a pre-Great Recession sample – September 1996 to December 2007. The latter ends at the same point in time as the BTZ sample. We report our empirical findings in Tables 10 to 13. These results are based on semi-annually aggregated excess returns and estimated for the one-month-ahead prediction horizon.[7] In this robustness study, we scale the cumulative excess returns; we use $r^e_{t \to t+6}/6$ as the predicted value and regress it on a one-month lagged predictive variable.

Full-sample simple predictive regression results are available in Table 10. Among VRP components, only the downside variance risk premium ($dvrp_t$) and skewness risk premium (srp_t) have slope parameters that are statistically different from zero and have adjusted R^2s comparable in magnitude with other pricing variables. Once we use $dvrp_t$ along with other pricing variables, we observe the following regularities in Table 11 which reports the following joint multi-variate regression results. First, the estimated slope parameter for $dvrp_t$ is statistically different from zero in all cases, except when we include srp_t. This result is not, however, surprising since srp_t and $dvrp_t$ are linearly dependent. Second, these regressions yield adjusted R^2s which range between 3.10% (for $dvrp_t$ and tms_t, in line with findings of BTZ that report weak predictability for tms_t) to 25.71% (for $dvrp_t$ and $infl_t$).[8] The downside variance risk premium in conjuncture with the variance risk premium or upside variance risk premium remains statistically significant and yields adjusted R^2s that are in the 7% neighborhood.

---

[7]A complete set of robustness checks, including monthly, quarterly, and annually aggregated excess returns results, are available in an online Appendix.

[8]The dynamics of inflation during the Great Recession period mimic the behavior of our variance risk premia. Gilchrist et al. (2014) meticulously study the behavior of this variable in the 2007-2009 period. According to their study, both full and matched PPI inflation in their model display an aggregate drop in 2008-2009, while the reaction of financially sound and weak firms are asymmetric, with the former lowering prices and the latter raising prices in this period. Thus, the predictive power of this variable, given the inherent asymmetric responses, is not surprising.

We obtain adjusted R^2s that are decidedly lower than those reported by BTZ for quarterly and annually aggregated multivariate regressions. These differences are driven by inclusion of the Great Recession period data in our full sample. To illustrate this point, we repeat our estimation with the data set ending in December 2007. Simple predictive regression results based on this data are available in Table 12. We immediately observe that exclusion of the Great Recession period data improves even the univariate predictive regression adjusted R^2s across the board. The estimated slope parameters are also closer to BTZ estimates and generally statistically significant.

In Table 13, we report multivariate regression results, based on 1996-2007 data. We notice that once $dvrp_t$ is included in the regression model, the variance risk premium, upside variance risk premium and skewness risk premium are no longer statistically significant. Other pricing variables, except for term spread, default spread, and inflation, yield slope parameters that are statistically significant. Thus, inflation seems to lack prediction power in this sub-sample. We do not observe statistically insignificant slope parameters for the downside variance risk premium except when we include vrp_t. Across the board, adjusted R^2s are high in this sub-sample.

4.6 Out-of-sample analysis

Our goal in this section is to compare the forecast ability of downside variance and skewness risk premia with common financial and macroeconomic variables used in equity premium predictability exercises.

To assess the ability of downside variance risk and skewness risk premia to forecast excess returns, we follow the literature on predictive accuracy tests. We assume a benchmark model (B) and a competitor model (C) in order to compare their predictive power for a given sample $\{y\}_{t=1}^T$. To generate k-period out-of-sample predictions $y_{t+k|t}$ for y_{t+k}, we split the total sample of T observations into in-sample and out-of-sample portions, where the first $1, \ldots, t_R$ in-sample observations are used to obtain the initial set of regression estimates. The out-of-sample observations span the last portion of the total sample $t = t_R + 1, \ldots, T$ and are used for forecast evaluation. The models are recursively estimated with the last in-sample observation ranging from $t = t_R$ to $t = T - k$, at each t forecasting $t + k$. That is, we use time t data to forecast the k-step ahead value. In our analysis, we use half of the total sample for the initial in-sample estimation, that is $t_R = \lfloor \frac{T}{2} \rfloor$ where

$\lfloor y \rfloor$ denotes the largest integer that is less than or equal to y. In order to generate subsequent sets of forecasts, we employ a recursive scheme (expanding window), even though the in-sample period can be fixed or rolling. The forecast errors from the two models are

$$\begin{aligned} e^{B}_{t+k|t} &= y_{t+k} - y^{B}_{t+k|t}, \\ e^{C}_{t+k|t} &= y_{t+k} - y^{C}_{t+k|t}, \end{aligned}$$

where $t = t_R, \ldots, T - k$. Thus, we obtain two sets of $t = T - t_R - k + 1$ recursive forecast errors.

The accuracy of each forecast is measured by a loss function $L(\bullet)$. Among the popular loss functions are the squared error loss $L(e_{t+k|t}) = (e_{t+k|t})^2$ and the absolute error loss $L(e_{t+k|t}) = |e_{t+k|t}|$. Let $d^{BC}_t = L(e_{t+k|t})^B - L(e_{t+k|t})^C$ be the error loss differential between the benchmark and competitor models, and denote the expectation operator by $\mathbb{E}(\bullet)$. To gauge if a model yields better forecasts than an alternative specification, a two-sided test may be run, where the null hypothesis is that the "two models have the same forecast accuracy" against the alternative hypothesis that the "two models have different forecast accuracy". Formally:

$$H_0 : \mathbb{E}(d^{BC}_t) = 0 \text{ vs. } H_A : \mathbb{E}(d^{BC}_t) \neq 0.$$

Alternatively, a one-sided test may be considered, where the null hypothesis is that "model C does not improve the forecast accuracy compared to model B" against the alternative hypothesis that "model C improves the forecast accuracy compared to model B". Formally:

$$H_0 : \mathbb{E}(d^{BC}_t) \leq 0 \text{ vs. } H_A : \mathbb{E}(d^{BC}_t) > 0.$$

In the context of our study, we apply forecast accuracy tests to non-nested models. The innovation of our analysis is to introduce two new predictors, the VRP^D and SRP. We compare the benchmark model B, which includes our proposed predictors, and the competitor C, which contains a traditional predictive variable such as the price-dividend ratio, dividend yield, price-earning ratio, etc. Failure to reject the null leads us to conclude that the classical predictor does not yield more accurate forecasts than our proposed predictor. Diebold and Mariano (1995) and West (1996) provide further inference results on this class of forecast accuracy tests.

4.7 Out-of-sample empirical findings

Following the influential study of Inoue and Kilian (2004), we first investigate the in-sample fit of the data by our proposed predictors – the VRP^D and SRP – and traditional predictors studied in the literature. Inoue and Kilian (2004) convincingly argue that to make dependable out-of-sample inference, we need reasonable in-sample fit. The second column of Table 14 reports adjusted R^2s for monthly, quarterly, and semi-annually aggregated excess returns regressed on our proposed and traditional predictors. These are in-sample results and no forecasting is performed. We notice that, first, for all predictors, adjusted R^2s improve with the prediction horizon. Second, we notice that for all predictors except Kelly and Pruitt's 2013 out-of-sample cross-sectional book-to-market index, adjusted R^2s are reasonably high. The Kelly-Pruitt index is by construction an out-of-sample predictor. Thus, the seemingly poor in-sample performance is not a cause for concern for us.

Once we establish the in-sample prediction power, we move to investigate out-of-sample forecast ability. Not surprisingly, out-of-sample adjusted R^2s – reported in the third column of Table 14 – are much smaller than their in-sample counterparts, with the exception of the Kelly-Pruitt index. This observation may be due to inclusion of data from the 2007-2009 Great Recession period in the out-of-sample exercise. As documented in Section 4.5, most predictors lose significant prediction power once data from this period is included in the analysis.

Our task is to investigate the relative forecast performance of our proposed downside and skewness risk premium measures against other well-known predictors. To this end, we implement the Diebold and Mariano (1995) (henceforth, DM) tests of prediction accuracy. The results of performing out-of-sample forecast accuracy tests are available in the fourth and the sixth column of Table 14, where we report DM test statistics, and in the fifth and the seventh columns of the same Table, where we report the associated p-values. We cannot reject the null of equal or superior forecast accuracy when the benchmark is the downside variance (or skewness) risk premium and the alternative model contains one of the traditional predictors, since p-values are greater than the conventional 5% test size. We note the following important considerations. First, these results are based on the DM forecast accuracy test for non-nested models. Our findings are robust for all the horizons we consider in our analysis (1, 3 and 6 months). Second, the null hypothesis states that the mean squared forecast error of the alternative model is larger than or equal to that of the benchmark model. This is a one-sided test, and negative DM statistics indicate that the alternative model performed worse than the benchmark model. Third, we interpret the p-values cautiously, following Boyer, Jacquier, and van Norden (2012). They point out that p-values are hard to interpret due to the Lindley-Smith paradox, and in addition, they need to be adjusted. To be precise, we produce multiple p-values in this analysis. Using unadjusted p-values in such an environment overstates the evidence against the null. Thus, following Boyer, Jacquier, and van Norden (2012), we apply a Bonferroni adjustment to the generated p-values. Our reported findings are, therefore, suitably conservative and reliable. Conventional competing variables such as the variance risk premium, price-dividend ratio, and price-earning ratio, have lower forecast accuracy than our proposed measures.

In a nutshell, the prediction power of the downside variance risk premium and skewness risk premium are not a figment of good in-sample fit of the data. In comparison with other pricing ratios and variables, our proposed measures have at least similar (and often superior) out-of-sample accuracy.

5   A Simple Equilibrium Model

Our goal in this section is to show that our empirical findings are supported by a simple equilibrium consumption-based asset pricing model. Our main objective is to highlight the roles that upside and downside variance play in pricing a risky asset in an otherwise standard asset pricing model. In particular, we show that under standard and mild assumptions, the weights and the signs attributed to upside and downside variances are inline with our empirical findings. To save space, we only report the main results. An online Appendix reports our derivations in great detail.

5.1   Preferences

We consider a endowment economy in discrete time. The representative agent's preferences over the future consumption stream are characterized by Kreps and Porteus (1978) intertemporal preferences, as formulated by Epstein and Zin (1989) and Weil (1989):

$$U_t = \left[(1 - \delta) C_t^{\frac{1-\gamma}{\theta}} + \delta \left(\mathbb{E}_t U_{t+1}^{1-\gamma} \right)^{\frac{1}{\theta}} \right]^{\frac{\theta}{1-\gamma}}, \tag{13}$$

where C_t is the consumption bundle at time t, δ is the subjective discount factor, γ is the coefficient of risk aversion, and ψ is the elasticity of intertemporal substitution (IES). Parameter θ is defined as $\theta \equiv \frac{1-\gamma}{1-\frac{1}{\psi}}$. If $\theta = 1$, then $\gamma = 1/\psi$ and EZ preferences collapse to expected power utility, which implies an agent who is indifferent to the timing of resolution of uncertainty of the consumption path. With $\gamma > 1/\psi$, the agent prefers early resolution of uncertainty. For $\gamma < 1/\psi$, the agent prefers late resolution of uncertainty. Epstein and Zin (1989) show that the logarithm of stochastic discount factor (SDF) implied by these preferences is given by:

$$\ln M_{t+1} = m_{t+1} = \theta \ln \delta - \frac{\theta}{\psi} \Delta c_{t+1} + (\theta - 1) r_{c,t+1}, \tag{14}$$

where $\Delta c_{t+1} = \ln \left(\frac{C_{t+1}}{C_t} \right)$ is the log growth rate of aggregate consumption, and $r_{c,t}$ is the log return of the asset that delivers aggregate consumption as dividends. This asset represents the returns on a wealth portfolio. The Euler equation states that

$$\mathbb{E}_t \left[\exp \left(m_{t+1} + r_{i,t+1} \right) \right] = 1, \tag{15}$$

where $r_{c,t}$ represents the log returns for the consumption generating asset $(r_{c,t})$. The risk-free rate, which represents the returns on an asset that delivers a unit of consumption in the next period with certainty, is defined as:

$$r_t^f = \ln \left[\frac{1}{\mathbb{E}_t(M_{t+1})} \right]. \tag{16}$$

5.2 Consumption Dynamics under the Physical Measure

Our specification of consumption dynamics incorporates elements from Bansal and Yaron (2004), Bekaert, Engstrom, and Ermolov (2014), and especially BTZ and Segal, Shaliastovich, and Yaron (2015).

Fundamentally, we follow Bansal and Yaron (2004) in assuming that consumption growth has a predictable component. We differ from Bansal and Yaron in assuming that the predictable component is proportional to consumption growth's upside and downside volatility components:[9]

$$\Delta c_{t+1} = \mu_0 + \mu_1 V_{u,t} + \mu_2 V_{d,t} + \sigma_c \left(\varepsilon_{u,t+1} - \varepsilon_{d,t+1} \right), \tag{17}$$

where $\varepsilon_{u,t+1}$ and $\varepsilon_{d,t+1}$ are two mean-zero shocks that affect both the realized and expected consumption growth.[10] $\varepsilon_{u,t+1}$ represents upside shocks to consumption growth, and $\varepsilon_{d,t+1}$ stands for downside shocks. Following Bekaert, Engstrom, and Ermolov (2014) and Segal, Shaliastovich, and Yaron (2015), we assume that these shocks follow a demeaned Gamma distribution and model them as

$$\varepsilon_{i,t+1} = \tilde{\varepsilon}_{i,t+1} - V_{i,t} \ \ i = \{u, d\}, \tag{18}$$

where $\tilde{\varepsilon}_{i,t+1} \sim \Gamma(V_{i,t}, 1)$. These distributional assumptions imply that volatilities of upside and downside shocks are time-varying and driven by shape parameters $V_{u,t}$ and $V_{d,t}$. In particular, we have that

$$Var_t[\varepsilon_{i,t+1}] = V_{i,t}, \ \ i = \{u, d\}. \tag{19}$$

Naturally, the total conditional variance of consumption growth when $\varepsilon_{u,t+1}$ and $\varepsilon_{d,t+1}$ are conditionally independent, is simply $\sigma_c^2 \left(V_{u,t} + V_{d,t} \right)$.

As a result, sign and size of μ_1 and μ_2 matter in this context. With $\mu_1 = \mu_2$, we have a stochastic volatility component in the conditional mean of consumption growth process, similar to the classic GARCH-in-Mean structure for modeling risk-return trade-off in equity returns. With both slope parameters equal to zero, the model yields the BTZ unpredictable consumption growth.[11] If $|\mu_1| = |\mu_2|$, with $\mu_1 > 0$ and $\mu_2 < 0$, we have Skewness-in-Mean, similar in spirit to Feunou,

---

[9]Segal, Shaliastovich, and Yaron (2015) maintain this assumption in their definition of the long-run risk component.

[10]This assumption is for the sake of brevity. Violating this assumption adds to algebraic complexity, but does not affect our analytical findings.

[11]It can be shown that assuming an unpredictable consumption growth process does not support the existence of distinct upside and downside variance risk premia that are supported by empirical evidence, if we assume agents endowed with Epstein and Zin (1989) preferences. In particular we have found that combining constant expected consumption growth with Epstein and Zin (1989) preferences will always yields positive upside variance risk-premium, which is in contradiction with our empirical findings. Using asymmetric preferences, such as smooth ambiguity aversion preferences of Klibanoff, Marinacci, and Mukerji (2009) or disappointment aversion of Gul (1991), it may be possible to derive plausible upside and downside variance risk premia for an economy with unpredictable consumption growth. The cost we pay is the loss of closed form analytical results. Miao, Wei, and Zhou (2012) use smooth ambiguity aversion preferences to motivate their study of variance risk premium, but assume time-variation in the conditional mean of the consumption growth.

Jahan-Parvar, and Tédongap (2013) formulation for equity returns. With $\mu_1 \neq \mu_2$, we have free parameters that have an impact on loadings of risk factors on risky asset returns and the stochastic discount factor. Both μ_1 and μ_2 are real-valued. Intuitively, we expect $\mu_1 > 0$: a rise in upside volatility at time t implies higher consumption growth at time $t + 1$, all else equal. By the same logic, we intuitively expect a negative-valued μ_2, implying an expected fall in consumption growth following an up-tick in downside volatility – following bad economic outcomes, households curb their consumption. In what follows, we buttress our intuition with theory and derive the analytical bounds on these parameters that ensure consistency with empirical facts.

We observe that

$$\ln \mathbb{E}_t \exp\left(\nu \varepsilon_{i,t+1}\right) = f(\nu)V_{i,t}, \tag{20}$$

where $f(\nu) = -(\ln(1 - \nu) + \nu)$. Both Bekaert, Engstrom, and Ermolov (2014) and Segal, Shaliastovich, and Yaron (2015) use this compact functional form for the Gamma-distribution cumulant. It simply follows that $f(\nu) > 0$, $f''(\nu) > 0$, and $f(\nu) > f(-\nu)$ for all $\nu > 0$.

We assume that $V_{i,t}$ follow a time-varying, square root process with time-varying volatility-of-volatility, similar to the specification of the volatility process in Bollerslev, Tauchen, and Zhou (2009):

$$V_{u,t+1} = \alpha_u + \beta_u V_{u,t} + \sqrt{q_{u,t}} z_{t+1}^u, \tag{21}$$

$$q_{u,t+1} = \gamma_{u,0} + \gamma_{u,1} q_{u,t} + \varphi_u \sqrt{q_{u,t}} z_{t+1}^1, \tag{22}$$

$$V_{d,t+1} = \alpha_d + \beta_d V_{d,t} + \sqrt{q_{d,t}} z_{t+1}^d, \tag{23}$$

$$q_{d,t+1} = \gamma_{d,0} + \gamma_{d,1} q_{d,t} + \varphi_d \sqrt{q_{d,t}} z_{t+1}^2, \tag{24}$$

where z_t^i are standard normal innovations, and $i = \{u, d, 1, 2\}$. The parameters must satisfy the following restrictions: $\alpha_u > 0, \alpha_d > 0, \gamma_{u,0} > 0, \gamma_{d,0} > 0, |\beta_u| < 1, |\beta_d| < 1, |\gamma_{u,1}| < 1, |\gamma_{d,1}| < 1, \varphi_u > 0, \varphi_d > 0$. In addition we assume that $\{z_t^u\}, \{z_t^d\}, \{z_t^1\}$, and $\{z_t^2\}$ are $i.i.d. \sim N(0, 1)$, and jointly independent from $\{\varepsilon_{u,t}\}$ and $\{\varepsilon_{d,t}\}$.

The assumptions above yield time-varying uncertainty and asymmetry in consumption growth. Through volatility-of-volatility processes $q_{u,t}$ and $q_{d,t}$, the set up induces additional temporal variation in consumption growth. Temporal variation in volatility-of-volatility process is necessary for generating sizable variance risk premium. Asymmetry is needed to generate upside and downside variance risk premia, as we show in what follows.

We solve the model following the same methodology proposed by Bansal and Yaron (2004), Bollerslev, Tauchen, and Zhou (2009), Segal, Shaliastovich, and Yaron (2015), and many others. We consider that the logarithm of wealth-consumption ratio w_t or price-consumption ratio ($pc_t = \ln\left(\frac{P_t}{C_t}\right)$) for the asset that pays the consumption endowment $\{C_{t+i}\}_{i=1}^{\infty}$, is affine with respect to state variables $V_{i,t}$ and $q_{i,t}$.

We then posit that the consumption-generating returns are approximately linear with respect to the log price-consumption ratio, as popularized by Campbell and Shiller (1988). That is:

$$r_{c,t+1} = \kappa_0 + \kappa_1 w_{t+1} - w_t + \Delta c_{t+1},$$

$$w_t = A_0 + A_1 V_{u,t} + A_2 V_{d,t} + A_3 q_{u,t} + A_4 q_{d,t},$$

where κ_0 and κ_1 are log-linearization coefficients and A_0, A_1, A_2, A_3 and A_4 are factor loading coefficients to be determined. We solve for the consumption-generating asset returns, $r_{c,t}$, using the Euler equation (15). Following standard arguments, we find the equilibrium values of coefficients A_0 to A_4:

$$A_1 = -\frac{f\left[\sigma_c(1-\gamma)\right] + (1-\gamma)\mu_1}{\theta(\kappa_1\beta_u - 1)}, \tag{25}$$

$$A_2 = -\frac{f\left[-\sigma_c(1-\gamma)\right] + (1-\gamma)\mu_2}{\theta(\kappa_1\beta_d - 1)}, \tag{26}$$

$$A_3 = \frac{(1-\kappa_1\gamma_{u,1}) - \sqrt{(1-\kappa_1\gamma_{u,1})^2 - \theta^2\varphi_u^2\kappa_1^4 A_1^2}}{\theta\kappa_1^2\varphi_u^2}, \tag{27}$$

$$A_4 = \frac{(1-\kappa_1\gamma_{d,1}) - \sqrt{(1-\kappa_1\gamma_{d,1})^2 - \theta^2\varphi_d^2\kappa_1^4 A_2^2}}{\theta\kappa_1^2\varphi_d^2}, \tag{28}$$

$$A_0 = \frac{\ln\delta + \left(1 - \frac{1}{\psi}\right)\mu_0 + \kappa_0 + \kappa_1\left(\alpha_u A_1 + \alpha_d A_2 + \gamma_{u,0} A_3 + \gamma_{d,0} A_4\right)}{1 - \kappa_1}. \tag{29}$$

It is easy to see that while A_3 and A_4 are negative-valued, the signs of A_1 and A_2 depend on signs and sizes of μ_1 and μ_2. We report the conditions that ensure $A_1 > 0$ and $A_2 < 0$ after introducing the dynamics of the model under the risk-neutral measure.

Standard algebraic manipulations yield the following representations for conditional equity premium and innovations of conditional equity premium:

$$
\begin{aligned}
r_{c,t+1} &= \ln\delta + \frac{\mu_0}{\psi} + \left[\frac{\mu_1}{\psi} - \frac{f\left[\sigma_c(1-\gamma)\right]}{\theta}\right]V_{u,t} + \left[\frac{\mu_2}{\psi} - \frac{f\left[-\sigma_c(1-\gamma)\right]}{\theta}\right]V_{d,t} \\
&\quad + \sigma_c(\varepsilon_{u,t+1} - \varepsilon_{d,t+1}) + (\kappa_1\gamma_{u,1} - 1)A_3 q_{u,t} + (\kappa_1\gamma_{d,1} - 1)A_4 q_{d,t} \qquad (30) \\
&\quad + \kappa_1\left[\left(A_1 z^u_{t+1} + \varphi_u A_3 z^1_{t+1}\right)\sqrt{q_{u,t}} + \left(A_2 z^d_{t+1} + \varphi_d A_4 z^2_{t+1}\right)\sqrt{q_{d,t}}\right],
\end{aligned}
$$

$$
\begin{aligned}
r_{c,t+1} - \mathbb{E}_t(r_{c,t+1}) &= \sigma_c(\varepsilon_{u,t+1} - \varepsilon_{d,t+1}) \\
&\quad + \kappa_1\left[\left(A_1 z^u_{t+1} + \varphi_u A_3 z^1_{t+1}\right)\sqrt{q_{u,t}} + \left(A_2 z^d_{t+1} + \varphi_d A_4 z^2_{t+1}\right)\sqrt{q_{d,t}}\right]. \quad (31)
\end{aligned}
$$

It is immediately obvious that there is significant correspondence between our characterization of risky returns and equation (10) of BTZ. The differences are driven by the different distributional assumptions regarding consumption growth shocks and the fact that we model upside and downside uncertainty explicitly rather than targeting aggregate uncertainty as in BTZ. Notice that $\left[-\frac{f[\sigma_c(1-\gamma)]}{\theta}\right] < \left[-\frac{f[-\sigma_c(1-\gamma)]}{\theta}\right]$ and both terms are positive-valued. Thus, the impact of $V_{u,t}$ and $V_{d,t}$ on expected returns depend on μ_1 and μ_2. We provide a crisp characterization of the equity premium to complete the analysis subsequently.

Due to differences in distributional assumptions, we do not follow BTZ or Bansal and Yaron methods for deriving equity premium and various variance risk premia. The dynamics specified so far are all under the physical measure ($\mathbb{P}$). We need to compute the dynamics under the risk-neutral measure ($\mathbb{Q}$) to derive the formulae for upside and downside variance risk premia and skewness risk premium.

5.3 Risk-Neutral Dynamics and the Premia

We derive the risk-neutral distribution of all the shocks, $\varepsilon_{u,t+1}$, $\varepsilon_{d,t+1}$, z^u_{t+1}, z^d_{t+1}, z^1_{t+1}, and z^2_{t+1}. Namely, we construct the characteristic functions of the shocks and exploit their salient properties to derive the expectations under the risk-neutral measure. Thus, our computations yield exact equity and risk premia measures, in contrast to approximate values reported by, for example, in equation (15) of Bollerslev, Tauchen, and Zhou (2009) or in Drechsler and Yaron (2011). Details of these derivations are available in the online Appendix.

The risk-neutral expectations of the upside and downside consumption shocks are

$$
\begin{aligned}
\mathbb{E}_t^{\mathbb{Q}}\left[\varepsilon_{u,t+1}\right] &= f'(-\gamma\sigma_c)V_{u,t} = -\frac{\gamma\sigma_c}{1+\gamma\sigma_c}V_{u,t}, \\
\mathbb{E}_t^{\mathbb{Q}}\left[\varepsilon_{d,t+1}\right] &= f'(\gamma\sigma_c)V_{d,t} = \frac{\gamma\sigma_c}{1-\gamma\sigma_c}V_{d,t}.
\end{aligned}
$$

Using a similar methodology, we characterize the risk-neutral distributions of Gaussian shocks z_{t+1}^u, z_{t+1}^d, z_{t+1}^1, and z_{t+1}^2:

$$
\begin{aligned}
z_{t+1}^u &\sim \mathbb{Q}N\left((\theta-1)\kappa_1 A_1\sqrt{q_{u,t}},1\right) \\
z_{t+1}^d &\sim \mathbb{Q}N\left((\theta-1)\kappa_1 A_2\sqrt{q_{d,t}},1\right) \\
z_{t+1}^1 &\sim \mathbb{Q}N\left((\theta-1)\kappa_1 A_3\varphi_u\sqrt{q_{u,t}},1\right) \\
z_{t+1}^2 &\sim \mathbb{Q}N\left((\theta-1)\kappa_1 A_4\varphi_d\sqrt{q_{d,t}},1\right).
\end{aligned}
$$

Any premium – whether equity, variance risk, or skewness risk premia – can be defined as the difference between the physical and risk-neutral expectations of processes. Hence, we commence computing the premia of interest, starting with the equity risk premium:

$$
\begin{aligned}
ERP_t &\equiv \mathbb{E}_t\left[r_{c,t+1}\right] - \mathbb{E}_t^{\mathbb{Q}}\left[r_{c,t+1}\right] \\
&= \kappa_1\left(\mathbb{E}_t\left[w_{t+1}\right] - \mathbb{E}_t^{\mathbb{Q}}\left[w_{t+1}\right]\right) + \mathbb{E}_t\left[\Delta c_{t+1}\right] - \mathbb{E}_t^{\mathbb{Q}}\left[\Delta c_{t+1}\right]. \qquad (32)
\end{aligned}
$$

It is clear from equation (32) that we need to compute both $\mathbb{E}_t\left[\Delta c_{t+1}\right] - \mathbb{E}_t^{\mathbb{Q}}\left[\Delta c_{t+1}\right]$ and $\mathbb{E}_t\left[w_{t+1}\right] - \mathbb{E}_t^{\mathbb{Q}}\left[w_{t+1}\right]$. It can be shown that:

$$
\mathbb{E}_t\left[\Delta c_{t+1}\right] - \mathbb{E}_t^{\mathbb{Q}}\left[\Delta c_{t+1}\right] = \gamma\sigma_c^2\left(\frac{1}{1+\gamma\sigma_c}V_{u,t} + \frac{1}{1-\gamma\sigma_c}V_{d,t}\right).
$$

Similarly:

$$
\begin{aligned}
\mathbb{E}_t\left[w_{t+1}\right] - \mathbb{E}_t^{\mathbb{Q}}\left[w_{t+1}\right] &= A_1\left(\mathbb{E}_t\left[V_{u,t}\right] - \mathbb{E}_t^{\mathbb{Q}}\left[V_{u,t}\right]\right) + A_2\left(\mathbb{E}_t\left[V_{d,t}\right] - \mathbb{E}_t^{\mathbb{Q}}\left[V_{d,t}\right]\right) \\
&\quad + A_3\left(\mathbb{E}_t\left[q_{u,t}\right] - \mathbb{E}_t^{\mathbb{Q}}\left[q_{u,t}\right]\right) + A_4\left(\mathbb{E}_t\left[q_{d,t}\right] - \mathbb{E}_t^{\mathbb{Q}}\left[q_{d,t}\right]\right).
\end{aligned}
$$

To compute $\mathbb{E}_t\left[w_{t+1}\right] - \mathbb{E}_t^{\mathbb{Q}}\left[w_{t+1}\right]$, we need the premia for each risk factor ($V_{u,t}, V_{d,t}, q_{u,t}$ and $q_{d,t}$). Straightforward algebra yields:

$$
\begin{aligned}
\mathbb{E}_t\left[V_{u,t}\right] - \mathbb{E}_t^{\mathbb{Q}}\left[V_{u,t}\right] &= (1-\theta)\kappa_1 A_1 q_{u,t}, \\
\mathbb{E}_t\left[V_{d,t}\right] - \mathbb{E}_t^{\mathbb{Q}}\left[V_{d,t}\right] &= (1-\theta)\kappa_1 A_2 q_{d,t}, \\
\mathbb{E}_t\left[q_{u,t}\right] - \mathbb{E}_t^{\mathbb{Q}}\left[q_{u,t}\right] &= (1-\theta)\kappa_1 A_3 \varphi_u^2 q_{u,t}, \\
\mathbb{E}_t\left[q_{d,t}\right] - \mathbb{E}_t^{\mathbb{Q}}\left[q_{d,t}\right] &= (1-\theta)\kappa_1 A_4 \varphi_d^2 q_{d,t}.
\end{aligned}
$$

Thus, it easily follows that the equity premium in our model is:

$$
ERP_t \equiv \frac{\gamma\sigma_c^2}{1+\gamma\sigma_c}V_{u,t} + \frac{\gamma\sigma_c^2}{1-\gamma\sigma_c}V_{d,t} + (1-\theta)\kappa_1\left(A_1^2 + A_3^2\varphi_u^2\right)q_{u,t} + (1-\theta)\kappa_1\left(A_2^2 + A_4^2\varphi_d^2\right)q_{d,t}. \tag{33}
$$

This expression for equity premium clearly shows that our model implies unequal loadings for upside and downside volatility factors. The slope coefficients for volatility-of-volatility factors are also – in general – unequal. We require that $\sigma_c < \frac{1}{\gamma}$ to maintain finite factor loadings.

We proceed and derive the closed form expressions for upside and downside variance risk premia. From equation (31) we know that

$$
\begin{aligned}
\sigma_{r,t}^2 &\equiv Var_t\left[r_{c,t+1}\right] \\
&= Var_t\left[\sigma_c(\varepsilon_{u,t+1} - \varepsilon_{d,t+1}) + \kappa_1\left[(A_1 z_{t+1}^u + \varphi_u A_3 z_{t+1}^1)\sqrt{q_{u,t}} + (A_2 z_{t+1}^d + \varphi_d A_4 z_{t+1}^2)\sqrt{q_{d,t}}\right]\right] \\
&= \sigma_c^2 V_{u,t} + \sigma_c^2 V_{d,t} + \kappa_1^2\left(A_1^2 + A_3^2\varphi_u^2\right)q_{u,t} + \kappa_1^2\left(A_2^2 + A_4^2\varphi_d^2\right)q_{d,t},
\end{aligned}
$$

where upside and downside variances are defined as:

$$\left(\sigma_{r,t}^u\right)^2 = \sigma_c^2 V_{u,t} + \kappa_1^2 \left(A_1^2 + A_3^2 \varphi_u^2\right) q_{u,t}, \tag{34}$$

$$\left(\sigma_{r,t}^d\right)^2 = \sigma_c^2 V_{d,t} + \kappa_1^2 \left(A_2^2 + A_4^2 \varphi_d^2\right) q_{d,t}. \tag{35}$$

Using the definition of variance risk premium, we compute the upside variance risk premium as:

$$\begin{aligned} VRP_t^U &\equiv \mathbb{E}_t^{\mathbb{Q}}\left[\left(\sigma_{r,t+1}^u\right)^2\right] - \mathbb{E}_t\left[\left(\sigma_{r,t+1}^u\right)^2\right], \\ &= (\theta - 1)\left(\sigma_c^2 \kappa_1 A_1 + \kappa_1^3 \left(A_1^2 + A_3^2 \varphi_u^2\right) A_3 \varphi_u^2\right) q_{u,t}. \end{aligned} \tag{36}$$

Similarly, we derive the following expression for the downside variance risk premium:

$$\begin{aligned} VRP_t^D &\equiv \mathbb{E}_t^{\mathbb{Q}}\left[\left(\sigma_{r,t+1}^d\right)^2\right] - \mathbb{E}_t\left[\left(\sigma_{r,t+1}^d\right)^2\right] \\ &= (\theta - 1)\left(\sigma_c^2 \kappa_1 A_2 + \kappa_1^3 \left(A_2^2 + A_4^2 \varphi_d^2\right) A_4 \varphi_d^2\right) q_{d,t}. \end{aligned} \tag{37}$$

Empirical evidences, presented in Section 4.4, imply $VRP_t^U < 0$ and $VRP_t^D > 0$, hence it follows that

$$\sigma_c^2 \kappa_1 A_1 + \kappa_1^3 \left(A_1^2 + A_3^2 \varphi_u^2\right) A_3 \varphi_u^2 > 0, \tag{38}$$

$$\sigma_c^2 \kappa_1 A_2 + \kappa_1^3 \left(A_2^2 + A_4^2 \varphi_d^2\right) A_4 \varphi_d^2 < 0. \tag{39}$$

Since $A_4 < 0$, $A_2 < 0$ is a sufficient condition for $\sigma_c^2 \kappa_1 A_2 + \kappa_1^3 \left(A_2^2 + A_4^2 \varphi_d^2\right) A_4 \varphi_d^2 < 0$. Moreover, $A_2 < 0 \Leftrightarrow \mu_2 < \dfrac{f\left[-\sigma_c(1-\gamma)\right]}{\gamma-1}$. In particular, $\mu_2 \leq 0 \Rightarrow A_2 < 0 \Rightarrow VRP_t^d > 0$. Since $A_3 < 0$, $A_1 > 0$ is a necessary condition for $\sigma_c^2 \kappa_1 A_1 + \kappa_1^3 \left(A_1^2 + A_3^2 \varphi_u^2\right) A_3 \varphi_u^2 > 0$. It is easily shown that

$$\sigma_c^2 \kappa_1 A_1 + \kappa_1^3 \left(A_1^2 + A_3^2 \varphi_u^2\right) A_3 \varphi_u^2 > 0 \Leftrightarrow A_1^L < A_1 < A_1^U$$

with

$$A_1^L = \frac{-\sigma_c^2 \kappa_1 + \sqrt{\sigma_c^4 \kappa_1^2 - 4\left(\kappa_1^3 A_3 \varphi_u^2\right)^2 A_3^2 \varphi_u^2}}{2\kappa_1^3 A_3 \varphi_u^2}, \quad A_1^U = \frac{-\sigma_c^2 \kappa_1 - \sqrt{\sigma_c^4 \kappa_1^2 - 4\left(\kappa_1^3 A_3 \varphi_u^2\right)^2 A_3^2 \varphi_u^2}}{2\kappa_1^3 A_3 \varphi_u^2}.$$

Both A_1^U and A_1^L are positive. In addition, it is easy to see that

$$A_1^L \; < \; A_1 < A_1^U \Leftrightarrow A_1^L < -\frac{f\left[\sigma_c(1-\gamma)\right] + (1-\gamma)\mu_1}{\theta(\kappa_1\beta_u - 1)} < A_1^U,$$

$$A_1^L \; < \; A_1 < A_1^U \Leftrightarrow \mu_1^L < \mu_1 < \mu_1^U,$$

with

$$\mu_1^L \; = \; \frac{f\left[\sigma_c(1-\gamma)\right] + \theta(\kappa_1\beta_u - 1)A_1^L}{\gamma - 1} > 0,$$

$$\mu_1^U \; = \; \frac{f\left[\sigma_c(1-\gamma)\right] + \theta(\kappa_1\beta_u - 1)A_1^U}{\gamma - 1} > 0,$$

which implies

$$\mu_1 > 0.$$

Consequently, confirming our earlier intuition, we find that for upside variance risk-premium to be negative, expected consumption growth must increases with the upside variance. Similarly, a non-positive relation between expected consumption growth and downside variance is sufficient to induce a positive downside variance risk-premium.

Next, we derive the closed form expression for the skewness risk premium. Following Feunou, Jahan-Parvar, and Tédongap (2013, 2014), we define the skewness as

$$sk_{r,t} = \left(\sigma_{r,t}^u\right)^2 - \left(\sigma_{r,t}^d\right)^2.$$

As a result, we calculate the skewness risk premium as

$$
\begin{aligned}
SRP_t \; &\equiv \; VRP_t^u - VRP_t^d \\
&= \; \left[\mathbb{E}_t^{\mathbb{Q}}\left[\left(\sigma_{r,t+1}^u\right)^2\right] - \mathbb{E}_t\left[\left(\sigma_{r,t+1}^u\right)^2\right]\right] - \left[\mathbb{E}_t^{\mathbb{Q}}\left[\left(\sigma_{r,t+1}^d\right)^2\right] - \mathbb{E}_t\left[\left(\sigma_{r,t+1}^d\right)^2\right]\right], \\
&= \; (\theta - 1)\left[\left(\sigma_c^2\kappa_1 A_1 + \kappa_1^3\left(A_1^2 + A_3^2\varphi_u^2\right)A_3\varphi_u^2\right)q_{u,t} - \left(\sigma_c^2\kappa_1 A_2 + \kappa_1^3\left(A_2^2 + A_4^2\varphi_d^2\right)A_4\varphi_d^2\right)q_{d,t}\right]. \quad (40)
\end{aligned}
$$

Based on our theoretical findings so far, it is easy to see that given $\theta < 0$ and conditions (38) and (39) – which we just verified – skewness risk premium is negative-valued, in compliance with our empirical findings in Section 4 and in Figure 7. Finally, since equation (33) implies that the equity risk-premium load positively on both $q_{u,t}$ and $q_{d,t}$, and because $VRP_t^U < 0$ is negatively proportional to $q_{u,t}$ and $VRP_t^D > 0$ is positively proportional to $q_{d,t}$, the equity risk-premium load positively on the downside variance risk-premium and negatively on the upside variance risk-premium, in compliance with our empirical findings in Section 4 and in Table 9. At this point, we have fully characterized the equity risk premium, upside and downside variance risk premia, the skewness risk premium, and by extension, risky asset returns.

In a nutshell, we show that first, our empirical findings are naturally aligned with a simple consumption-based asset pricing model. Second, the assumptions needed to support our empirical results are mild – we require distinct and time-varying upside and downside shocks to the consumption growth process, a predictable component in conditional consumption growth proportional to these up and down shocks variances, and an affine loading on risk factors. These are commonly maintained assumptions in the variance risk premium literature. Given these assumptions, we show that the upside variance risk premium is smaller in absolute term than the downside variance risk premium, that both upside and downside variance risk premia have opposite signs, and that the skewness risk premium is a negative-valued quantity.

6 Conclusion

In this study, we have decomposed the celebrated variance risk premium of Bollerslev, Tauchen, and Zhou (2009) – arguably one of the most successful short-term predictors of excess equity returns – to show that its prediction power stems from the downside variance risk premium embedded in this measure. Market participants seem more concerned with market downturns and demand a premium for bearing that risk. By contrast, they seem to like upward uncertainty in the market. As a result, the downside variance risk premium – the difference between option-implied, risk-neutral expectations of market downside volatility and historical, realized downside variances – demonstrates significant prediction power (that is at least as powerful as the variance risk premium and often stronger) for excess returns.

We also show that the difference between upside and downside variance risk premia – our proposed measure of the skewness risk premium – is both a priced factor in equity markets and a powerful predictor of excess returns. The skewness risk premium performs well for intermediate prediction steps beyond the reach of short-run predictor such as downside variance risk or variance risk premia and long-term predictors such as price-dividend or price-earning ratios alike. The skewness risk premium constructed from one-month's worth of data predicts excess returns between 8 months to a year ahead. The same measure constructed from a quarter's worth of data, predicts monthly excess returns between 4 months to one year ahead.

Our findings demonstrate remarkable robustness to the inclusion of common pricing variables. Downside variance risk and skewness risk premia have similar or better out-of-sample forecast ability in comparison with common pricing factors.

Finally, we show that our results are compatible with a simple equilibrium consumption-based asset pricing model. We develop a model where consumption growth features separate upside and downside time-varying shock processes, with feedback from volatilities to future growth. We show that under mild requirements about consumption growth, upside, and downside volatility processes, we can characterize the equity premium, upside and downside variance risk premia, and the skewness risk premium that support the main stylized facts obtained from our empirical investigation. In particular, we observe unequal weights for upside and downside variances in the equity premium, and opposite signs for upside and downside variance risk premia.

References

Amaya, D., P. Christoffersen, K. Jacobs, and A. Vasquez. 2013. Does realized skewness predict the cross-section of equity returns? *Working Paper, UQAM, Rotman School of Management - University of Toronto, C.T. Bauer College of Business - University of Houston, and ITAM School of Business* .

Amengual, D., and D. Xiu. 2014. Resoution of policy uncertainty and sudden declines in volatility. *Working Paper, CEMFI and Chicago Booth* .

Andersen, T. G., T. Bollerslev, F. X. Diebold, and H. Ebens. 2001a. The distribution of realized stock return volatility. *Journal of Financial Economics* 61:43–76.

Andersen, T. G., T. Bollerslev, F. X. Diebold, and P. Labys. 2001b. The distribution of realized exchange rate volatility. *Journal of the American Statistical Association* 96:42–55.

———. 2003. Modeling and forecasting realized volatility. *Econometrica* 71:579–625.

Andersen, T. G., and O. Bondarenko. 2007. *Volatility as an asset class*, chap. Construction and Interpretation of Model-Free Implied Volatility, 141–81. London, U.K.: Risk Books.

Andersen, T. G., O. Bondarenko, and M. T. Gonzalez-Perez. 2014. Exploring return dynamics via corridor implied volatility. *Working Paper* .

Ang, A., and G. Bekaert. 2007. Stock return predictability: Is it there? *Review of Financial Studies* 20:651–707.

Bakshi, G., N. Kapadia, and D. Madan. 2003. Stock return characteristics, skew laws and the differential pricing of individual equity options. *Review of Financial Studies* 16:101–43.

Bandi, F. M., and R. Renò. 2014. Price and volatility co-jumps. *Journal of Financial Economics, forthcoming* .

Bansal, R., and A. Yaron. 2004. Risks for the long run: A potential resolution of asset pricing puzzles. *Journal of Finance* 59:1481–1509.

Barndorff-Nielsen, O. E., S. Kinnebrock, and N. Shephard. 2010. *Volatility and time series econometrics: Essays in honor of robert f. engle*, chap. Measuring downside risk: realised semivariance, 117–36. Oxford University Press.

Bekaert, G., E. Engstrom, and A. Ermolov. 2014. Bad environments, good environments: A non-gaussian asymmetric volatility model. *Journal of Econometrics, forthcoming* .

Bollerslev, T., G. Tauchen, and H. Zhou. 2009. Expected stock returns and variance risk premia. *Review of Financial Studies* 22:4463–92.

Bollerslev, T., and V. Todorov. 2011a. Estimation of jump tails. *Econometrica* 79:1727–83.

———. 2011b. Tails, fears and risk premia. *Journal of Finance* 66:2165–211.

Boyer, M. M., E. Jacquier, and S. van Norden. 2012. Are underwriting cycles real and forecastable? *The Journal of Risk and Insurance* 79:995–1015.

Campbell, J. Y., and R. J. Shiller. 1988. The dividend-price ratio and expectations of future dividends and discount factors. *Review of Financial Studies* 1:195–228.

Carr, P., and D. Madan. 1998. *Volatility*, chap. Towards a Theory of Volatility Trading, 417–27. Risk Publications.

———. 1999. Option valuation using the fast fourier transform. *Journal of Computational Finance* 2:61–73.

———. 2001. *Quantitative analysis of financial markets*, vol. 2, chap. Determining Volatility Surfaces and Option Values from an Implied Volatility Smile, 163–91. World Scientific Press.

Chang, B., P. Christoffersen, and K. Jacobs. 2013. Market skewness risk and the cross-section of stock returns. *Journal of Financial Economics* 107:46–68.

Cochrane, J. H. 1991. Production-based asset pricing and the link between stock returns and economic fluctuations. *Journal of Finance* 46:209–37.

Colacito, R., E. Ghysels, and J. Meng. 2014. Skewness in expected macro fundamentals and the predictability of equity returns: Evidence and theory. *Working Paper, Kenan Flagler Business School, UNC Chapel Hill* .

Corsi, F. 2009. A simple approximate long-memory model of realized volatility. *Journal of Financial Econometrics* 7:174–96.

Diebold, F. X., and R. S. Mariano. 1995. Comapring predictive accuracy. *Journal of Business and Economic Statistics* 13:253–63.

Dionne, G., J. Li, and C. Okou. 2014. An extension of the consumption-based CAPM model. *Working Paper, HEC Montréal, Lingnan University, and UQAM* .

Drechsler, I., and A. Yaron. 2011. Whats Vol got to do with it? *Review of Financial Studies* 24:1–45.

Eeckhoudt, L., and H. Schlesinger. 2008. Changes in risk and the demand for saving. *Journal of Monetary Economics* 55:1329 – 1336.

Epstein, L. G., and S. E. Zin. 1989. Substitution, risk aversion, and the temporal behavior of consumption and asset returns: A theoretical framework. *Econometrica* 57:937–69.

Fama, E. F., and K. R. French. 1988. Dividend yields and expected stock returns. *Journal of Financial Economics* 22:3–25.

———. 1989. Business conditions and expected returns on stocks and bonds. *Journal of Financial Economics* 25:23–49.

Feunou, B., J.-S. Fontaine, A. Taamouti, and R. Tédongap. 2014. Risk premium, variance premium, and the maturity structure of uncertainty. *Review of Finance* 18:219–69.

Feunou, B., M. R. Jahan-Parvar, and R. Tédongap. 2013. Modeling Market Downside Volatility. *Review of Finance* 17:443–81.

———. 2014. Which parametric model for conditional skewness? *European Journal of Finance, forthcoming* .

Ghysels, E., A. Plazzi, and R. Valkanov. 2011. Conditional Skewness of Stock Market Returns in Developed and Emerging Markets and its Economic Fundamentals. *Working Paper, Kenan-Flagler Business School-UNC, and Rady School of Business-UCSD* .

Gilchrist, S., R. Schoenle, J. W. Sim, and E. Zakrajšek. 2014. Inflation dynamics during the financial crisis. *Working Paper, Federal Reserve Board and Boston University* .

Goyal, A., and I. Welch. 2008. A comprehensive look at the empirical performance of equity premium prediction. *Review of Financial Studies* 21:1455–508.

Groeneveld, R., and G. Meeden. 1984. Measuring skewness and kurtosis. *The Statistician* 33:391–9.

Gul, F. 1991. A Teory of Disappointment Aversion. *Econometrica* 59:667–86.

Hansen, P. R., and A. Lunde. 2006. Realized variance and market microstructure noise. *Journal of Business and Economic Statistics* 24:127–61.

Harvey, C. R., and A. Siddique. 1999. Autoregressive Conditional Skewness. *Journal of Financial and Quantitative Analysis* 34:465–88.

———. 2000. Conditional Skewness in Asset Pricing Tests. *Journal of Finance* 55:1263–95.

Hodrick, R. J. 1992. Dividend yields and expected stock returns: Alternative procedures for inference and measurement. *Review of Financial Studies* 5:357–386.

Inoue, A., and L. Kilian. 2004. In-sample or out-of-sample tests of predictability: Which one shouldf we use? *Econometric Reviews* 23:371–402.

Jacquier, E., and C. Okou. 2014. Disentangling continuous volatility from jumps in long-run risk-return relationships. *Journal of Financial Econometrics* 12:544–83.

Kelly, B. T., and H. Jiang. 2014. Tail risk and asset prices. *Review of Financial Studies* 27:2841–71.

Kelly, B. T., and S. Pruitt. 2013. Market expectations in the cross section of present values. *Journal of Finance* 68:1721–56.

Kim, T.-H., and H. White. 2004. On More Robust Estimation of Skewness and Kurtosis. *Finance Research Letters* 1:56–73.

Klibanoff, P., M. Marinacci, and S. Mukerji. 2009. Recursive smooth ambiguity preferences. *Journal of Economic Theory* 144:930–76.

Kozhan, R., A. Neuberger, and P. Schneider. 2014. The skew risk premium in the equity index market. *Review of Financial Studies* 26:2174–203.

Kreps, D. M., and E. L. Porteus. 1978. Temporal Resolution of Uncertainty and Dynamic Choice Theory. *Econometrica* 46:185–200.

Lettau, M., and S. Ludvigson. 2001. Consumption, aggregate wealth, and expected stock returns. *Journal of Finance* 56:815–50.

Ludvigson, S. C., and S. Ng. 2009. Macro factors in bond risk premia. *Review of Financial Studies* 22:5027–67.

Miao, J., B. Wei, and H. Zhou. 2012. Ambiguity aversion and variance premium. *Working Paper, Federal Reserve Board and Boston University* .

Nakamura, E., J. Steinsson, R. Barro, and J. Ursúa. 2013. Crises and recoveries in an empirical model of consumption disasters. *American Economic Journal: Macroeconomics* 5:35–74.

Neuberger, A. 2012. Realized skewness. *Review of Financial Studies* 25:3423–55.

Segal, G., I. Shaliastovich, and A. Yaron. 2015. Good and bad uncertainty: Macroeconomic and financial market implications. *Journal of Financial Economics, forthcoming* .

Weil, P. 1989. The equity premium puzzle and the risk-free rate puzzle. *Journal of Monetary Economics* 24:401–21.

West, K. D. 1996. Asymptotic inference about predictive ability. *Econometrica* 64:1067–84.

Table 1: **Summary Statistics**

	Mean (%)	Median (%)	Std. Dev. (%)	Skewness	Kurtosis	AR(1)
Panel A: Excess Returns						
Equity	1.9771	14.5157	20.9463	-0.1531	10.5559	-0.0819
Equity (1996-2007)	3.0724	12.5824	17.6474	-0.1379	5.9656	-0.0165
Panel B: Risk-Neutral						
Variance	19.3544	18.7174	6.6110	1.5650	7.6100	0.9897
Downside Variance	16.9766	16.2104	5.8727	1.6746	8.0637	0.9880
Upside Variance	9.2570	9.1825	3.1295	1.1479	6.0030	0.9885
Skewness	-7.7196	-7.0090	3.0039	-2.0380	9.6242	0.9679
Panel C: Realized						
Variance	19.2776	18.1475	8.7583	2.0683	8.7517	0.9998
Downside Variance	13.5841	12.7362	6.2639	2.0297	8.6130	0.9998
Upside Variance	13.6748	12.9029	6.1295	2.1022	8.8680	0.9998
Skewness	0.0907	0.1186	0.4124	-0.3292	2.7632	0.9694
Panel D: Risk Premium						
Variance	0.0768	0.8349	4.7214	-1.3578	7.5797	0.9802
Downside Variance	3.3925	3.3805	3.5259	-0.0114	5.9518	0.9684
Upside Variance	-4.4178	-3.3486	3.7281	-2.4339	10.6756	0.9909
Skewness	-7.8103	-6.9824	2.9213	-2.1850	10.3067	0.9668

This table reports the summary statistics for the quantities investigated in this study. Mean, median, and standard deviation values are annualized and in percentages. We report excess kurtosis values. $AR(1)$ represents the values for the first autocorrelation coefficient. The full sample is September 1996 to December 2010. We also consider a sub-sample ending in December 2007.

Table 2: S&P 500 Index Option Data

	OTM Put			OTM Call			
	$\underline{S}/S < 0.97$	$0.97 < \underline{S}/S < 0.99$	$0.99 < \underline{S}/S < 1.01$	$1.01 < \underline{S}/S < 1.03$	$1.03 < \underline{S}/S < 1.05$	$\underline{S}/S > 1.05$	All
Panel A: By Moneyness							
Number of contracts	223,579	57,188	71,879	57,522	26,154	100,121	536,443
Average price	15.08	39.44	39.67	38.47	21.97	15.50	23.90
Average implied volatility	25.68	17.05	15.88	15.58	14.30	16.31	20.06
	$DTM < 30$	$30 < DTM < 60$	$60 < DTM < 90$	$90 < DTM < 120$	$120 < DTM < 150$	$DTM > 150$	All
Panel B: By Maturity							
Number of contracts	115,392	140,080	83,937	36,163	22,302	138,569	536,443
Average price	10.45	14.90	20.17	24.88	26.20	45.82	23.90
Average implied volatility	19.40	20.20	20.06	21.11	20.48	20.13	20.06
	$VIX < 15$	$15 < VIX < 20$	$20 < VIX < 25$	$25 < VIX < 30$	$30 < VIX < 35$	$VIX > 35$	All
Panel C: By VIX Level							
Number of contracts	74,048	115,970	164,832	88,146	37,008	56,439	536,443
Average price	17.90	20.70	24.89	26.84	26.80	28.93	23.90
Average implied volatility	11.63	15.92	19.42	22.20	25.31	34.72	20.06

This table sorts S&P 500 index option data by moneyness, maturity, and VIX level. Out-of-the-money (OTM) call and put options from OptionMetrics from September 3, 1996 to December 30, 2010 are used. The moneyness is measured by the ratio of the strike price ($\underline{S}$) to underlying asset price (S). DTM is the time to maturity in number of calendar days. The average price and the average implied volatility are expressed in dollars and percentages, respectively.

Table 3: Relationship between Variance Risk Premium Components and Financial and Macroeconomic Variables

Variance Risk Premium			Downside Variance Risk Premium		
Variable	t-Stat	R^2	Variable	t-Stat	R^2
Nonfarm Payrolls, Total Private	11.44	41.94	Nonfarm Payrolls, Total Private	7.67	24.52
Nonfarm Payrolls, Wholesale Trade	10.55	38.06	IPI, Durable Goods Materials	7.08	21.70
IPI, Durable Goods Materials	9.61	33.79	Nonfarm Payrolls, Wholesale Trade	6.99	21.26
Nonfarm Payrolls, Transportation, Trade & Utilities	9.16	31.69	Industrial Production Index, Total Index	6.81	20.40
Nonfarm Payrolls, Services	8.90	30.46	IPI, Final Products and Nonindustrial Supplies	6.62	19.47
IPI, Manufacturing (SIC)	8.27	27.45	IPI, Manufacturing (SIC)	6.57	19.25
IPI, Final Products and Nonindustrial Supplies	8.20	27.08	Nonfarm Payrolls, Transportation, Trade & Utilities	6.39	18.41
Nonfarm Payrolls, Retail Trade	8.16	26.89	Nonfarm Payrolls, Services	6.25	17.77
Industrial Production Index, Total Index	7.96	25.92	Nonfarm Payrolls, Retail Trade	5.84	15.84
Nonfarm Payrolls, Construction	7.80	25.15	IPI, Final Products	5.73	15.37

Upside Variance Risk Premium			Skewness Risk Premium		
Variable	t-Stat	R^2	Variable	t-Stat	R^2
Nonfarm Payrolls, Total Private	14.24	52.82	PPI, Intermediate Materials, Supplies & Components	-5.92	16.23
Nonfarm Payrolls, Wholesale Trade	13.41	49.85	Nonfarm Payrolls, Mining and Logging	-5.67	15.09
Nonfarm Payrolls, Transportation, Trade & Utilities	10.94	39.82	Nonfarm Payrolls, Construction	-5.26	13.24
IPI, Durable Goods Materials	10.67	38.61	Nonfarm Payrolls, Wholesale Trade	-5.11	12.61
Nonfarm Payrolls, Services	10.66	38.56	1-Year Treasury	-5.06	12.39
Nonfarm Payrolls, Construction	10.38	37.31	CPI, All Items	-4.98	12.03
Nonfarm Payrolls, Retail Trade	9.51	33.33	CPI, All Items Less Medical Care	-4.95	11.94
IPI, Manufacturing (SIC)	8.49	28.50	6-Month Treasury Bill	-4.92	11.80
IPI, Final Products and Nonindustrial Supplies	8.31	27.63	Nonfarm Payrolls, Total Private	-4.88	11.63
Nonfarm Payrolls, Financial Sector	8.01	26.18	CPI, All Items Less Food	-4.82	11.36

This table reports the ten macroeconomic variables that demonstrate high contemporaneous correlation and explanatory power for variance and skewness risk premia. The results are sorted based on the size of adjusted R^2s from performing a univariate, linear regression analysis where the dependent variable is either the variance risk premium, upside variance risk premium, downside variance risk premium, or skewness risk premium, and the independent variable is one of the 124 macroeconomic and financial variable series studied by Feunou et al. (2014). Both adjusted R^2s and Student's t-statistic for the slope parameters are reported.

Table 4: Policy News Potentially Associated with Volatility Changes–Booth Dates

Date	ΔVariance	ΔReturn	News
08/18/98	-0.373 (-0.365)	0.013	President Clinton admits to "wrong" relationship with Ms. Lewinsky and FOMC's decision to leave interest rates unchanged
09/01/98	-0.722 (-0.664)	0.035	Fed adds money to the banking system with Repo.
09/08/98	-0.526 (-0.455)	0.021	Fed Chairman Greenspan's statement that a rate cut might be forthcoming.
09/14/98	-0.185	0.027	President Clinton advocated a coordinated global policy for economic growth in NYC.
09/23/98	-0.344 (-0.280)	0.027	Fed Chairman Greenspan testimony before the Committee on the Budget, U.S. Senate.
10/20/98	-0.253	-0.007	3 big US banks delivered better-than-expected earnings and bullish mood after Fed rate cut previous week.
08/11/99	-0.266 (-0.276)	0.008	Fed Beige Book release shows that US economic growth remains strong.
01/07/00	-0.500	0.031	Unemployment report shows the lowest unemployment rate in the past 30 years.
03/16/00	-0.266	0.037	Release of Inflation Remains Tame Enough to Keep the Federal Reserve from Tightening Credit
04/17/00	-0.373 (-0.296)	0.032	Treasury Secretary Lawrence H. Summers Statement that Fundamentals of Economy are in Place
10/19/00	-0.241	0.018	Feds Greenspan Gives Keynote Speech at Cato Institute and Jobless Claim Drop by 7,000 in Latest Week
01/03/01	-0.282 (-0.179)	0.052	Fed's Announcement of a Surprise, Inter-Meeting Rate Cut
05/17/05	-0.275 (-0.303)	0.01	John Snow Call on China to Take An Intermediate Step in Revaluing its Currency
05/19/05	-0.297		Fed Chairman A. Greenspan Steps up Criticism of Fannie Mae and Freddie Mac
06/15/06	-0.549 (-0.625)	0.017	Fed Chairman B. Bernankes Speech on Inflation Expectations within Historical Ranges
06/29/06	-0.295 (-0.325)	0.016	FOMC Statement to Raise Its Target for the Federal Funds Rate by 25 Basis Points
07/19/06	-0.272		Fed Chairman B. Bernanke Warned that the Fed Must Guard Against Rising Prices Taking Hold
02/28/07	-0.396		Fed Chairman B. Bernanke Told a House Panel that Markets Seemed Working Well
03/06/07	-0.217		Henry Paulson in Tokyo Said the Global Economy was As Strong As He's Ever Seen
06/27/07	-0.271		FOMC Announcement Generated Market Rebound the Previous Date
08/21/07	-0.188		Senator Dodd said the Fed to Deal with the Turmoil after Meeting with Paulson and Bernanke
09/18/07	-0.415 (-0.353)	0.024	FOMC Decided to Lower its Target for the Federal Funds Rate by 50 Basis Points
03/18/08	-0.216		Fed Cut the Fed Funds Rate by Three-Quarters of a Percentage Point
10/14/08	-0.489 (-0.304)	-0.048	FOMC Decided to Lower its Target for the Federal Funds Rate by 50 Basis Points
10/20/08	-0.426 (-0.413)	0.033	Fed Chairman B. Bernanke Testimony on the Budget, U.S. House of Representatives
10/28/08	-0.313 (-0.230)	0.075	Fed to Cut the Rate Following the Two-Day FOMC Meeting is Expected by the Market
11/13/08	-0.328 (-0.240)	0.062	President Bush's Speech on Financial Crisis
12/19/08	-0.244		President Bush Declared that TARP Funds to be Spent on Programs Paulson Deemed Necessary
02/24/09	-0.261		President Obama's First Speech as the President to Joint Session of U.S. Congress
05/10/10	-0.647 (-0.601)	0.003	European Policy Makers Unveiled An Unprecedented Emergency Loan Plan
03/21/11	-0.277		Japanese Nuclear Reactors Cooled Down and Situations in Libya Tamed by Unilateral Forces
08/09/11	-0.433 (-0.370)	0.046	FOMC Statement Explicitly Stating A Duration for An Exceptionally Low Target Rate
10/27/11	-0.245 (-0.205)	0.034	European Union Leaders Made a Bond Deal to Fix the Greek Debt Crisis
01/02/13	-0.432 (-0.427)	0.025	President Obama and Senator McConnell's Encouraging Comments on the "Fiscal Cliff" Issue

This table from Amengual and Xiu (2014) presents in the last column the events that may lead to the largest volatility drops in sample. The first column is the date of the event. The second shows changes in estimated spot variance, whereas the third column is the returns of the index on the corresponding days.

Table 5: **Reaction of Variance and Skewness Risk Premia to Financial and Macroeconomic Announcements**

Booth Date	ΔVar	Δr	VRP		VRP^U		VRP^D		SRP	
			Change	Level	Change	Level	Change	Level	Change	Level
08/18/1998	-0.373	0.013	-0.0146	0.0964	-0.0059	-0.0045	-0.0132	0.1188	-0.0073	0.1234
09/01/1998	-0.722	0.035	-0.0292	0.1432	-0.0206	0.0066	-0.0210	0.1666	-0.0004	0.1600
09/08/1998	-0.526	0.021	-0.0404	0.1190	-0.0189	-0.0123	-0.0348	0.1498	-0.0159	0.1621
09/23/1998	-0.344	0.027	-0.0131	0.0980	-0.0105	-0.0241	-0.0088	0.1337	0.0017	0.1578
10/20/1998	-0.253	-0.007	-0.0160	0.0444	-0.0143	-0.0453	-0.0100	0.0875	0.0043	0.1328
08/11/1999	-0.266	0.008	-0.0169	0.0540	-0.0123	-0.0223	-0.0124	0.0815	-0.0001	0.1038
01/07/2000	-0.5	0.031	-0.0305	0.0137	-0.0028	-0.0341	-0.0328	0.0429	-0.0300	0.0770
03/16/2000	-0.266	0.037	-0.0174	-0.0209	-0.0118	-0.0553	-0.0130	0.0164	-0.0012	0.0717
04/17/2000	-0.373	0.032	-0.0183	0.0023	-0.0134	-0.0527	-0.0132	0.0426	0.0003	0.0953
10/19/2000	-0.241	0.018	-0.0190	0.0027	-0.0088	-0.0412	-0.0164	0.0340	-0.0076	0.0752
01/03/2001	-0.282	0.052	-0.0229	-0.0137	-0.0242	-0.0616	-0.0110	0.0285	0.0131	0.0900
05/17/2005	-0.275	0.01	-0.0063	0.0178	-0.0023	-0.0202	-0.0059	0.0372	-0.0036	0.0575
06/15/2006	-0.549	0.017	-0.0251	0.0201	-0.0141	-0.0260	-0.0209	0.0423	-0.0068	0.0683
06/29/2006	-0.295	0.016	-0.0154	0.0035	-0.0100	-0.0332	-0.0121	0.0275	-0.0021	0.0607
09/18/2007	-0.415	0.024	-0.0272	0.0059	-0.0100	-0.0357	-0.0252	0.0344	-0.0152	0.0701
10/14/2008	-0.489	-0.048	-0.0040	0.0054	-0.0106	-0.0730	0.0032	0.0641	0.0138	0.1371
10/20/2008	-0.426	0.033	-0.0628	-0.0012	-0.0280	-0.0943	-0.0558	0.0688	-0.0278	0.1631
10/28/2008	-0.313	0.075	-0.0518	0.0380	-0.0311	-0.1027	-0.0402	0.1187	-0.0091	0.2214
11/13/2008	-0.328	0.062	-0.0412	0.0071	-0.0253	-0.1270	-0.0322	0.0986	-0.0069	0.2256
05/10/2010	-0.647	0.003	-0.0631	0.0764	-0.0386	-0.0215	-0.0488	0.1058	-0.0102	0.1273
08/09/2011	-0.433	0.046	-0.0628	0.0754	-0.0365	-0.0143	-0.0504	0.0997	-0.0139	0.1140
10/27/2011	-0.245	0.034	-0.0240	-0.0447	-0.0184	-0.0953	-0.0165	0.0115	0.0019	0.1068

This table reports the reaction of the variance risk premium (VRP), upside variance risk premium (VRP^U), downside variance risk premium (VRP^D), and skewness risk premium (SRP) to the macroeconomic and financial news documented in Table 4. The table reports changes in conditional volatility (ΔVar) and S&P 500 returns (Δr) on the event day, as well as changes and levels of VRP, VRP^U, VRP^D and SRP on the event date. A negative sign in the change of a risk premium signifies a decline on the arrival of a particular macroeconomic or financial announcement. A positive sign implies the opposite.

Table 6: **Predictive Content of Premium Measure**

h	1		3		6		12	
	t-Stat	$\bar{R}^2$	t-Stat	$\bar{R}^2$	t-Stat	$\bar{R}^2$	t-Stat	$\bar{R}^2$
k	Panel A: Variance Risk Premium							
1	2.43	2.61	2.51	2.83	1.02	0.02	0.68	-0.30
2	2.84	3.76	3.42	5.58	1.50	0.68	1.04	0.05
3	4.11	8.13	3.58	6.18	1.78	1.19	1.56	0.78
6	2.78	3.65	2.24	2.22	1.57	0.82	2.09	1.87
9	1.98	1.65	1.94	1.57	1.47	0.66	1.98	1.64
12	1.96	1.64	1.43	0.61	1.53	0.77	1.73	1.14
k	Panel B: Downside Variance Risk Premium							
1	2.57	2.99	2.68	3.30	1.27	0.34	0.95	-0.06
2	3.22	4.92	4.08	7.95	2.07	1.78	1.54	0.74
3	4.76	10.72	4.46	9.50	2.61	3.12	2.32	2.37
6	3.72	6.75	3.42	5.70	2.84	3.85	3.21	4.98
9	2.96	4.27	3.14	4.86	2.82	3.86	2.99	4.35
12	3.04	4.60	2.65	3.39	2.81	3.86	2.80	3.84
k	Panel C: Upside Variance Risk Premium							
1	2.08	1.79	1.91	1.44	0.44	-0.44	-0.04	-0.55
2	2.15	1.96	2.15	1.96	0.39	-0.47	-0.18	-0.54
3	3.05	4.41	2.07	1.79	0.26	-0.52	-0.27	-0.52
6	1.57	0.82	0.61	-0.36	-0.40	-0.48	-0.27	-0.53
9	0.83	-0.18	0.36	-0.50	-0.52	-0.42	-0.14	-0.57
12	0.74	-0.27	-0.05	-0.59	-0.33	-0.52	-0.41	-0.49
k	Panel D: Skewness Risk Premium							
1	-0.10	-0.55	0.41	-0.46	0.96	-0.04	1.25	0.30
2	0.61	-0.35	1.67	0.98	1.98	1.59	2.16	1.98
3	1.03	0.04	2.24	2.18	2.81	3.70	3.29	5.17
6	2.27	2.30	3.33	5.38	4.05	8.00	4.45	9.59
9	2.57	3.13	3.39	5.70	4.20	8.73	3.98	10.59
12	2.83	3.95	3.43	5.93	3.88	7.60	4.07	8.34

This table reports predictive regression results for prediction horizons (k) between 1 and 12 months ahead, and aggregation levels (h) between 1 and 12 months, based on a predictive regression model of the form $r_{t \to t+k} = \beta_0 + \beta_1 x_t(h) + \varepsilon_{t \to t+k}$. In this regression model, $r_{t \to t+k}$ is the cumulative excess returns between t and $t + k$, $x_t(h)$ is the proposed variance or skewness risk premia component that takes the values from variance risk, upside variance risk, downside variance risk, or skewness risk premia measures, and $\varepsilon_{t \to t+k}$ is a zero-mean error term. The reported Student's t-statistics for slope parameters are constructed from heteroscedasticity and serial correlation consistent standard errors that explicitly take account of the overlap in the regressions, following Hodrick (1992). $\bar{R}^2$ represents adjusted R^2s.

Table 7: **Predictive Content of Risk-Neutral Measure**

h	1		3		6		12	
	t-Stat	$\bar{R}^2$	t-Stat	$\bar{R}^2$	t-Stat	$\bar{R}^2$	t-Stat	$\bar{R}^2$
k			Panel A: Risk-Neutral Variance					
1	0.28	-0.51	0.50	-0.41	0.69	-0.29	0.75	-0.24
2	1.14	0.17	1.24	0.30	1.35	0.44	1.39	0.51
3	1.30	0.38	1.52	0.72	1.83	1.28	2.13	1.92
6	2.10	1.88	2.33	2.43	2.76	3.57	3.21	4.95
9	2.32	2.44	2.55	3.05	2.95	4.22	3.15	4.85
12	2.21	2.20	2.45	2.82	2.89	4.11	3.30	5.45
k			Panel B: Risk-Neutral Downside Variance					
1	0.27	-0.51	0.57	-0.37	0.77	-0.23	0.87	-0.14
2	1.22	0.27	1.39	0.51	1.49	0.66	1.54	0.74
3	1.42	0.56	1.70	1.04	2.03	1.70	2.35	2.44
6	2.23	2.17	2.52	2.91	2.97	4.21	3.42	5.67
9	2.43	2.71	2.68	3.42	3.10	4.70	3.26	5.22
12	2.32	2.48	2.55	3.09	2.99	4.42	3.42	5.84
k			Panel C: Risk-Neutral Upside Variance					
1	0.29	-0.50	0.27	-0.51	0.36	-0.48	0.20	-0.53
2	0.93	-0.07	0.76	-0.23	0.78	-0.21	0.60	-0.35
3	0.99	-0.02	0.94	-0.06	1.04	0.05	1.00	0.00
6	1.74	1.12	1.72	1.09	1.92	1.48	2.05	1.77
9	2.01	1.71	2.09	1.89	2.31	2.42	2.38	2.59
12	1.90	1.49	2.09	1.92	2.45	2.83	2.57	3.17
k			Panel D: Risk-Neutral Skewness					
1	0.22	-0.52	0.87	-0.14	1.10	0.11	1.27	0.34
2	1.51	0.70	2.02	1.67	2.06	1.76	2.08	1.79
3	1.93	1.48	2.47	2.74	2.85	3.80	3.13	4.65
6	2.70	3.42	3.28	5.21	3.80	7.02	4.11	8.18
9	2.76	3.64	3.17	4.92	3.64	6.54	3.56	6.26
12	2.67	3.44	2.88	4.07	3.27	5.35	3.66	6.73

This table reports predictive regression results for risk-neutral variance and skewness measures. The predictive regression model, prediction horizons, aggregation levels, and notation are the same as in the results reported in Table 6. The difference is in the definition of $x_t(h)$: instead of risk premia, we use risk-neutral measures for variance, upside variance, downside variance, and skewness.

Table 8: **Predictive Content of Realized (Physical) Measure**

h	1		3		6		12	
	t-Stat	$\bar{R}^2$	t-Stat	$\bar{R}^2$	t-Stat	$\bar{R}^2$	t-Stat	$\bar{R}^2$
k			Panel A: Realized Variance					
1	-1.10	0.12	-0.99	-0.01	-0.10	-0.55	0.09	-0.55
2	-0.67	-0.30	-0.86	-0.15	0.18	-0.54	0.40	-0.47
3	-1.18	0.22	-0.75	-0.25	0.36	-0.48	0.62	-0.34
6	0.01	-0.57	0.48	-0.44	1.13	0.15	1.07	0.09
9	0.55	-0.40	0.78	-0.22	1.33	0.44	1.12	0.15
12	0.49	-0.45	0.98	-0.02	1.27	0.35	1.40	0.56
k			Panel B: Realized Downside Variance					
1	-1.05	0.06	-0.90	-0.10	-0.08	-0.55	0.09	-0.55
2	-0.53	-0.40	-0.76	-0.23	0.21	-0.53	0.39	-0.47
3	-1.04	0.05	-0.68	-0.30	0.39	-0.48	0.59	-0.36
6	0.05	-0.57	0.48	-0.44	1.08	0.10	0.99	-0.01
9	0.54	-0.41	0.75	-0.25	1.21	0.27	1.01	0.01
12	0.44	-0.48	0.89	-0.12	1.14	0.18	1.30	0.40
k			Panel C: Realized Upside Variance					
1	-1.15	0.18	-1.09	0.10	-0.13	-0.54	0.10	-0.55
2	-0.82	-0.18	-0.95	-0.05	0.14	-0.54	0.41	-0.46
3	-1.33	0.43	-0.82	-0.18	0.34	-0.49	0.66	-0.32
6	-0.05	-0.57	0.48	-0.44	1.17	0.21	1.16	0.19
9	0.39	-0.41	0.81	-0.19	1.44	0.61	1.23	0.29
12	0.54	-0.42	1.08	0.09	1.39	0.54	1.51	0.74
k			Panel D: Realized Skewness					
1	0.44	-0.45	1.58	0.81	0.63	-0.33	-0.06	-0.55
2	1.51	0.70	1.67	0.99	0.96	-0.05	-0.26	-0.52
3	1.45	0.61	1.19	0.23	0.71	-0.28	-0.89	-0.12
6	0.54	-0.40	0.11	-0.56	-1.01	0.01	-2.64	3.25
9	0.07	-0.58	-0.54	-0.41	-3.01	4.41	-3.67	6.67
12	-0.55	-0.41	-1.82	1.33	-3.37	5.70	-3.36	5.67

This table reports predictive regression results for realized variance and skewness measures. The predictive regression model, prediction horizons, aggregation levels, and notation are the same as in the results reported in Table 6. The difference is in the definition of $x_t(h)$: instead of risk premia, we use realized (historical) measures for variance, upside variance, downside variance, and skewness.

Table 9: **Joint Regression Results**

h	1			3			6			12		
	t-Stat		$\bar{R}^2$	*t*-Stat		$\bar{R}^2$	*t*-Stat		$\bar{R}^2$	*t*-Stat		$\bar{R}^2$
k	Up	Down		Up	Down		Up	Down		Up	Down	
Panel A: Risk Premium												
1	-0.01	1.49	2.45	-0.12	1.86	2.77	-0.58	1.32	-0.03	-0.85	1.27	-0.21
2	-0.78	2.49	4.72	-1.28	3.66	8.28	-1.38	2.46	2.26	-1.54	2.17	1.49
3	-1.28	3.79	11.04	-1.81	4.32	10.63	-2.06	3.33	4.84	-2.34	3.31	4.77
6	-2.46	4.19	9.36	-3.00	4.56	9.80	-3.31	4.39	8.98	-3.14	4.54	9.54
9	-2.75	3.99	7.76	-3.10	4.45	9.36	-3.46	4.49	9.50	-2.74	4.09	7.83
12	-3.06	4.29	9.06	-3.18	4.18	8.30	-3.13	4.24	8.61	-2.97	4.10	8.06
Panel B: Risk-Neutral Measures												
1	0.08	-0.01	-1.06	-1.13	1.24	-0.22	-1.30	1.46	0.15	-1.48	1.70	0.51
2	-1.00	1.27	0.27	-2.42	2.69	3.10	-2.27	2.61	2.90	-2.00	2.45	2.35
3	-1.59	1.89	1.39	-2.92	3.26	5.01	-3.22	3.68	6.55	-2.87	3.59	6.21
6	-1.64	2.14	3.09	-2.93	3.47	6.89	-3.25	3.99	9.12	-2.61	3.79	8.66
9	-1.32	1.88	3.12	-2.02	2.62	5.09	-2.25	3.05	6.88	-1.42	2.62	5.78
12	-1.35	1.89	2.94	-1.49	2.07	3.77	-1.39	2.18	4.93	-1.28	2.55	6.20
Panel C: Realized (Physical) Measures												
1	-0.63	0.42	-0.28	-1.82	1.72	1.17	-0.69	0.68	-0.84	0.11	-0.10	-1.10
2	-1.62	1.50	0.51	-1.92	1.83	1.24	-0.93	0.95	-0.60	0.48	-0.46	-0.90
3	-1.68	1.46	1.05	-1.41	1.34	0.25	-0.62	0.64	-0.82	1.27	-1.24	-0.02
6	-0.54	0.54	-0.97	-0.01	0.06	-1.01	1.39	-1.31	0.61	3.54	-3.49	6.14
9	0.01	0.08	-0.99	0.72	-0.64	-0.54	3.61	-3.52	6.77	4.82	-4.76	11.39
12	0.63	-0.55	-0.83	2.07	-1.98	1.77	3.99	-3.91	8.24	4.66	-4.59	11.22

This table reports predictive regression results when multiple variance components (risk premia, risk-neutral, and realized measures) are included in the regression model. The prediction horizons, aggregation levels, and notation are the same as in the results reported in Table 6. The difference is in the regression model. Both upside and downside variance components are in the model: $r_{t \to t+k} = \beta_0 + \beta_1 x_{1,t}(h) + \beta_2 x_{2,t}(h) + \varepsilon_{t \to t+k}$. $x_{1,t}(h)$ pertains to upside measures and $x_{2,t}(h)$ represents the downside measures used in the analysis.

Table 10: **Semi-annual Simple Predictive Regressions, Sep. 1996 to Dec. 2010**

	(1)	(2)	(3)	(4)	(5)	(6)	(7)	(8)	(9)	(10)	(11)	(12)
$Intercept$	0.0005	-0.0026	-0.0132	0.0012	0.0756	0.0861	0.0514	0.0004	-0.0000	0.0210	-0.0105	-0.0093
	(0.1995)	(-1.1632)	(-3.0304)	(0.7230)	(2.9076)	(3.1978)	(2.0974)	(0.1293)	(-0.0067)	(6.3627)	(-3.1169)	(-2.0903)
$uvrp_t$	-0.0179											
	(-0.3917)											
$dvrp_t$		0.1135										
		(2.5900)										
srp_t			-0.1838									
			(-3.6007)									
vrp_t				0.0516								
				(1.4937)								
$log(p_t/d_t)$					-0.0419							
					(-2.8630)							
$log(p_{t-1}/d_t)$						-0.0478						
						(-3.1550)						
$log(p_t/e_t)$							-0.0384					
							(-2.0487)					
tms_t								0.7181				
								(0.4233)				
dfs_t									1.6755			
									(0.3885)			
$infl_t$										-0.8052		
										(-6.7137)		
$kpis_t$											0.1472	
											(4.0170)	
$kpos_t$												0.1203
												(2.5798)
$Adj.\ R^2(\%)$	-0.5157	3.3439	6.7611	0.7406	4.1793	5.1472	1.9009	-0.5000	-0.5172	21.0807	8.4028	3.3140

This table presents predictive regressions of the semi-annually (scaled) cumulative excess return $r_{t \to t+6}^e = \sum_{j=1}^{6} r_{t+j}^e / 6$ on each one-period (1-month) lagged predictor from September 1996 to December 2010.

Table 11: **Semi-annual Multiple Predictive Regressions, Sep. 1996 to Dec. 2010**

	(1)	(2)	(3)	(4)	(5)	(6)	(7)	(8)	(9)	(10)	(11)
$Intercept$	-0.0128	-0.0128	-0.0133	0.0787	0.0951	0.0582	-0.0045	-0.0084	0.0171	-0.0137	-0.0131
	(-2.9375)	(-2.9375)	(-2.9489)	(3.0953)	(3.6144)	(2.4206)	(-1.3553)	(-1.7752)	(4.9989)	(-3.8625)	(-2.8590)
$uvrp_t$	-0.1545										
	(-2.7123)										
$dvrp_t$	0.2100	0.0555	0.4321	0.1272	0.1392	0.1309	0.1178	0.1359	0.1289	0.1048	0.1129
	(3.7629)	(1.1549)	(3.4605)	(2.9688)	(3.2550)	(2.9980)	(2.6638)	(2.9172)	(3.3499)	(2.4918)	(2.6228)
srp_t		-0.1545									
		(-2.7123)									
vrp_t			-0.2640								
			(-2.7177)								
$log(p_t/d_t)$				-0.0462							
				(-3.2112)							
$log(p_{t-1}/d_t)$					-0.0557						
					(-3.7277)						
$log(p_t/e_t)$						-0.0471					
						(-2.5413)					
tms_t							1.2900				
							(0.7681)				
dfs_t								6.2346			
								(1.3864)			
$infl_t$									-0.8272		
									(-7.0977)		
$kpis_t$										0.1425	
										(3.9439)	
$kpos_t$											0.1197
											(2.6128)
$Adj.\ R^2(\%)$	6.9505	6.9505	6.9664	8.5372	10.3900	6.4572	3.1016	3.8843	25.7111	11.2225	6.6602

This table presents predictive regressions of the semi-annually (scaled) cumulative excess return $r^e_{t \to t+6}/6 = \sum_{j=1}^6 r^e_{t+j}/6$ on one-period (1-month) lagged downside variance risk premium $dvrp$ and one alternative predictor in turn from September 1996 to December 2010.

54

Table 12: Semi-annual Simple Predictive Regressions, Sep. 1996 to Dec. 2007

$Intercept$	0.0129	-0.0070	-0.0124	0.0014	0.2016	0.2164	0.0913	0.0035	0.0206	0.0052	-0.0059	-0.0047
	(5.1388)	(-3.5015)	(-2.6470)	(1.0794)	(6.6115)	(7.0123)	(3.9851)	(1.5568)	(3.4844)	(1.0608)	(-2.2330)	(-1.3202)
$uvrp_t$	0.2679											
	(4.5558)											
$dvrp_t$		0.2784										
		(6.6863)										
srp_t			-0.2156									
			(-3.5176)									
vrp_t				0.2300								
				(6.5106)								
$log(p_t/d_t)$					-0.1092							
					(-6.5085)							
$log(p_{t-1}/d_t)$						-0.1176						
						(-6.9106)						
$log(p_t/e_t)$							-0.0662					
							(-3.8474)					
tms_t								-0.1990				
								(-0.1295)				
dfs_t									-25.6836			
									(-3.0118)			
$infl_t$										-0.0735		
										(-0.4029)		
$kpis_t$											0.1217	
											(4.0782)	
$kpos_t$												0.0940
												(2.4679)
$Adj.\ R^2(\%)$	13.2802	25.3069	8.1025	24.2902	24.2781	26.6030	9.6656	-0.7680	5.8882	-0.6536	10.8080	3.7964

This table presents predictive regressions of the semi-annually (scaled) cumulative excess return $r^e_{t \to t+6}/6 = \sum_{j=1}^{6} r^e_{t+j}/6$ on each one-period (1-month) lagged predictor from September 1996 to December 2007.

Table 13: Semi-annual Multiple Predictive Regressions, Sep. 1996 to Dec. 2007

	(1)	(2)	(3)	(4)	(5)	(6)	(7)	(8)	(9)	(10)	(11)
$Intercept$	-0.0045 (-1.0099)	-0.0045 (-1.0099)	-0.0049 (-1.0492)	0.1736 (6.6158)	0.1954 (7.5813)	0.1053 (5.7055)	-0.0087 (-3.2688)	-0.0033 (-0.4896)	-0.0142 (-2.8139)	-0.0155 (-5.8453)	-0.0162 (-4.7195)
$uvrp_t$	0.0454 (0.6200)										
$dvrp_t$	0.2554 (4.5711)	0.3008 (5.4521)	0.2065 (1.4127)	0.2534 (7.0696)	0.2629 (7.6580)	0.3156 (8.4728)	0.2853 (6.7545)	0.2669 (5.7833)	0.2980 (6.8848)	0.2716 (6.9931)	0.2847 (7.0767)
srp_t		0.0454 (0.6200)									
vrp_t			0.0632 (0.5133)								
$log(p_t/d_t)$				-0.0990 (-6.8974)							
$log(p_{t-1}/d_t)$					-0.1113 (-7.8692)						
$log(p_t/e_t)$						-0.0855 (-6.1130)					
tms_t							1.3106 (0.9772)				
dfs_t								-4.9164 (-0.5838)			
$infl_t$									0.2541 (1.5553)		
$kpis_t$										0.1148 (4.5066)	
$kpos_t$											0.1050 (3.2382)
$Adj.\ R^2(\%)$	24.9460	24.9460	24.8746	45.2343	49.3937	41.8336	25.2805	24.9203	26.1258	35.0975	30.4605

This table presents predictive regressions of the semi-annually (scaled) cumulative excess return $r^e_{t \to t+6}/6 = \sum_{j=1}^{6} r^e_{t+j}/6$ on one-period (1-month) lagged downside variance risk premium $dvrp$ and one alternative predictor in turn from September 1996 to December 2007.

Table 14: **Out-of-Sample Analysis**

	Adj. $R^2(\%)$ for IS	Adj. $R^2(\%)$ for OOS	dvrp vs. x_t		srp vs. x_t	
			DM	p-value	DM	p-value
		Panel A: One Month				
$dvrp_t$	4.6723	0.6347			-0.0426	0.5170
srp_t	3.4862	-0.6055	0.0426	0.4830		
vrp_t	3.7175	-0.1087	-0.0271	0.5108	-0.0374	0.5149
$log(p_t/d_t)$	6.3871	-1.1465	-0.3716	0.6449	-0.4769	0.6833
$log(p_{t-1}/d_t)$	6.7059	-1.1123	-0.2414	0.5954	-0.3453	0.6351
$log(p_t/e_t)$	4.2430	-0.9384	0.2572	0.3985	0.2930	0.3848
$kpos_t$	-1.0697	2.0261	1.3282	0.0921	1.7998	0.0359
		Panel B: Three Months				
$dvrp_t$	24.6956	5.5674			0.0895	0.4644
srp_t	21.3847	-0.8775	-0.0895	0.5356		
vrp_t	19.8333	4.6494	0.3654	0.3574	0.2742	0.3919
$log(p_t/d_t)$	16.8502	-1.0456	0.5398	0.2947	0.6162	0.2689
$log(p_{t-1}/d_t)$	18.4235	-0.5345	0.5425	0.2937	0.6304	0.2642
$log(p_t/e_t)$	11.2493	0.2510	0.9778	0.1641	1.0725	0.1417
$kpos_t$	-0.6580	0.6473	1.7537	0.0397	1.8782	0.0302
		Panel C: Six Months				
$dvrp_t$	35.4498	0.1580			-1.2144	0.8877
srp_t	20.0010	2.3028	1.2144	0.1123		
vrp_t	31.7578	2.7778	-0.4553	0.6756	-1.0558	0.8545
$log(p_t/d_t)$	28.2580	0.4752	0.3393	0.3672	-1.2086	0.8866
$log(p_{t-1}/d_t)$	32.1452	1.2361	0.2877	0.3868	-1.2333	0.8913
$log(p_t/e_t)$	17.2860	1.0359	0.8114	0.2086	-0.6382	0.7383
$kpos_t$	2.9373	12.1162	1.7801	0.0375	1.2382	0.1078

This table presents the out-of-sample performance of predictors to forecast monthly ($r^e_{t \to t+1}$ in the top panel), quarterly ($r^e_{t \to t+3}/3$ in the middle panel) and semi-annually ($r^e_{t \to t+6}/6$ in the bottom panel) scaled cumulative excess returns, with observations spanning September 1996 to December 2010. The first two columns present the adjusted R^2 (%) for the in-sample (IS) and out-of-sample (OOS) observations, that is the first and last half fractions of the data. The columns headed "$dvrp$ vs. x_t" test the null hypothesis that "an alternative predictor (x_t) does not yield a better forecast than the downside variance risk premium ($dvrp$)". The columns headed "srp vs. x_t" test the null hypothesis that "an alternative predictor (x_t) does not yield a better forecast than the skewness risk premium (srp)". The reported test statistics and p-values are computed from the Diebold and Mariano (1995) model comparison procedure. Note that the Bonferroni adjustment is required when multiple p-values are produced, to avoid overstating the evidence against the null. Thus, to maintain an overall significance level of 5% (resp. 10%), one should adjust each individual test size to 0.0083 = 5%/6 (resp. 0.0167 = 10%/6) since 6 tests are performed for a given horizon.

Figure 1: S&P 500 Put and Call Contracts per Day

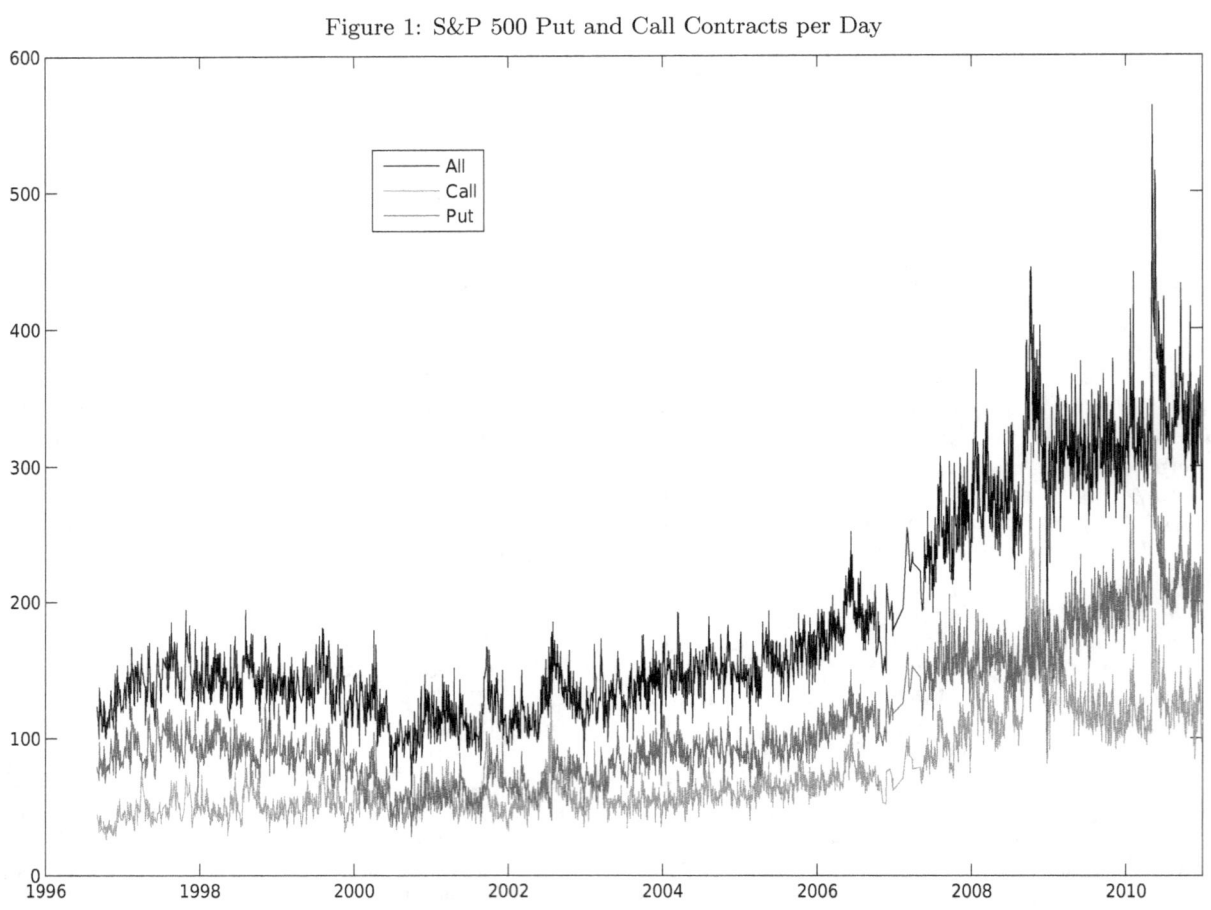

This graph show the number of outstanding put and call contracts written on the S&P 500 index per day for the 1996-2010 period. In addition, it plots the sum of put and call contract numbers. Source: OptionMetrics Ivy DB accessed via WRDS.

Figure 2: The Term-Structure of Risk Neutral Variance

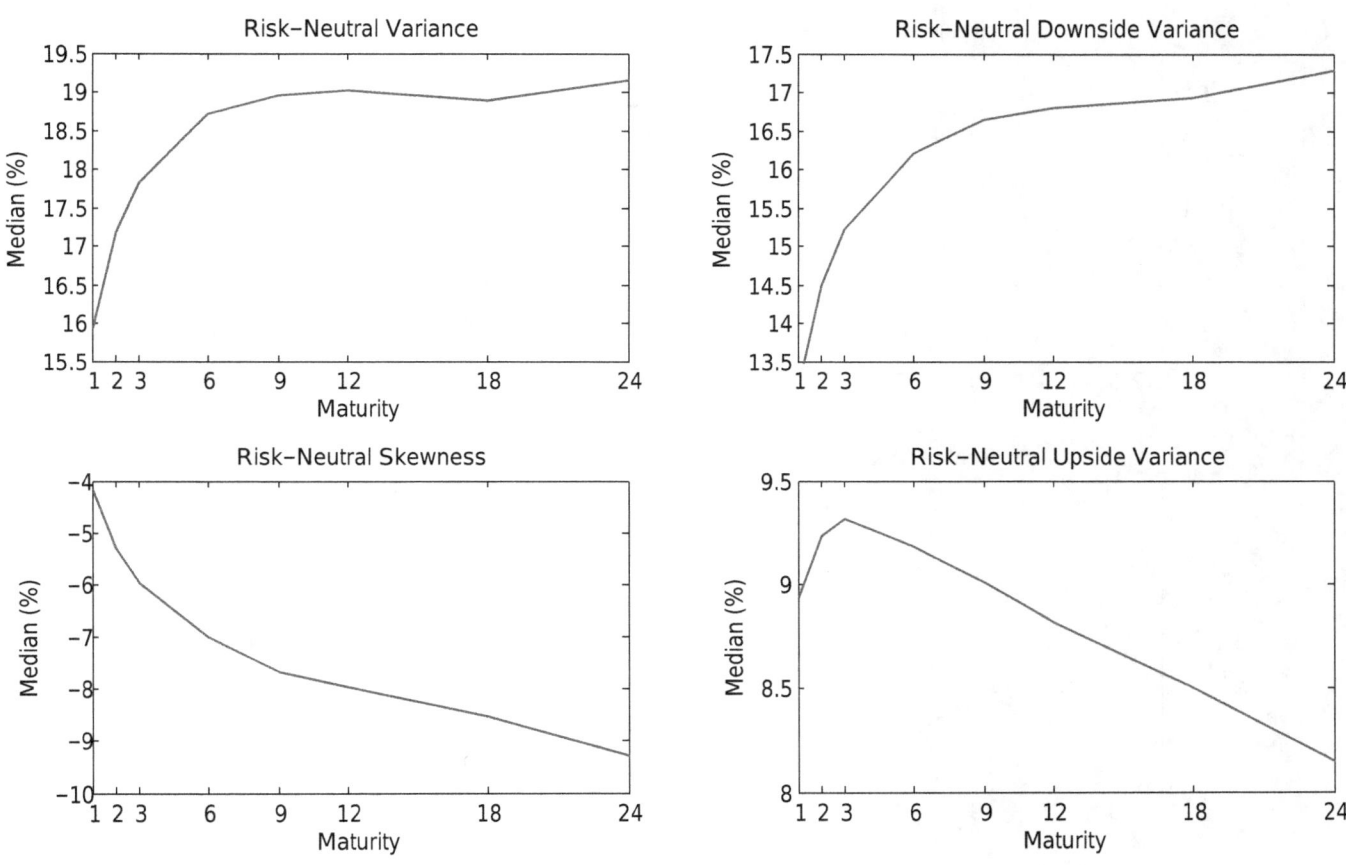

Figure 3: The Term-Structure of Realized Variance

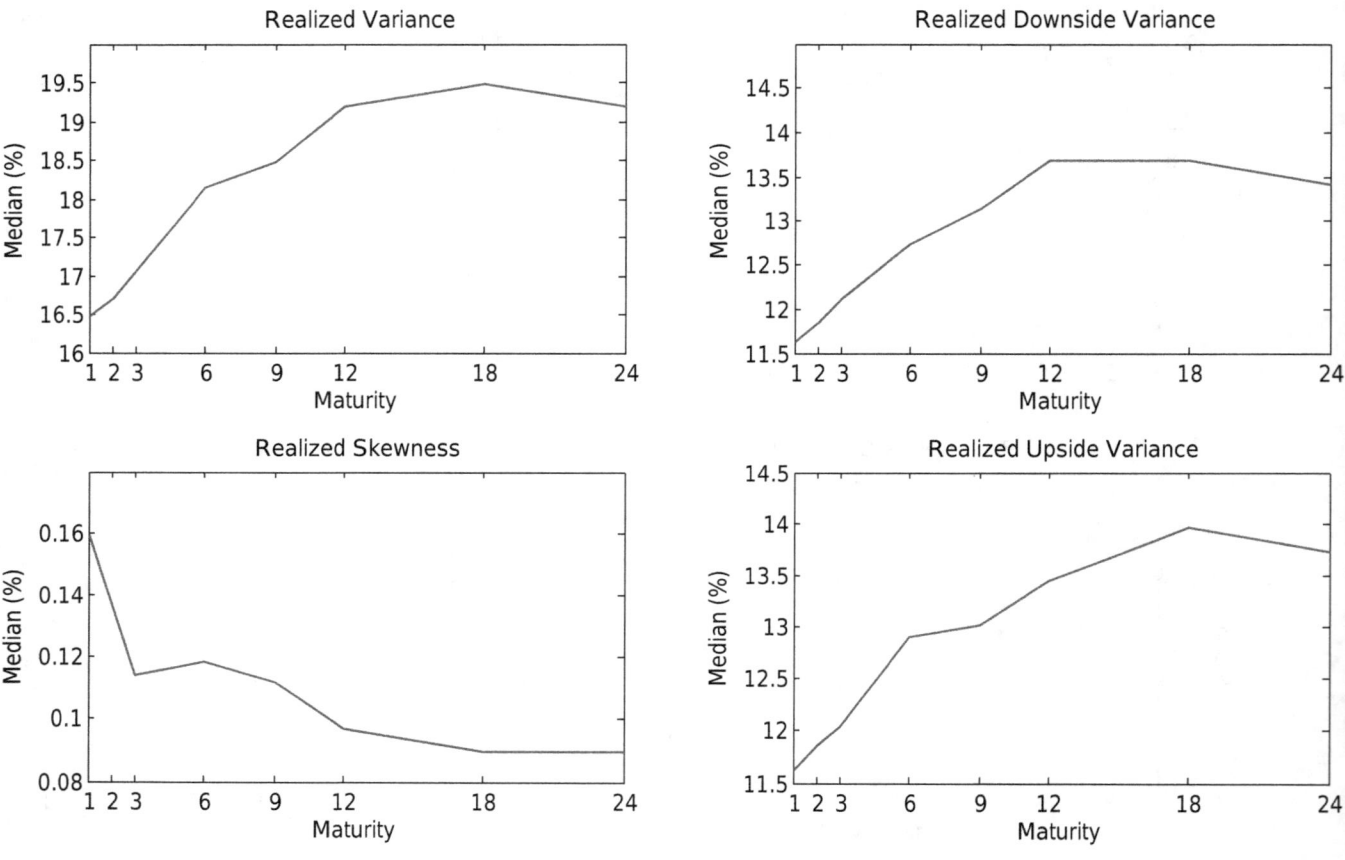

Figure 4: Student's t-Statistics for Predictive Regressions

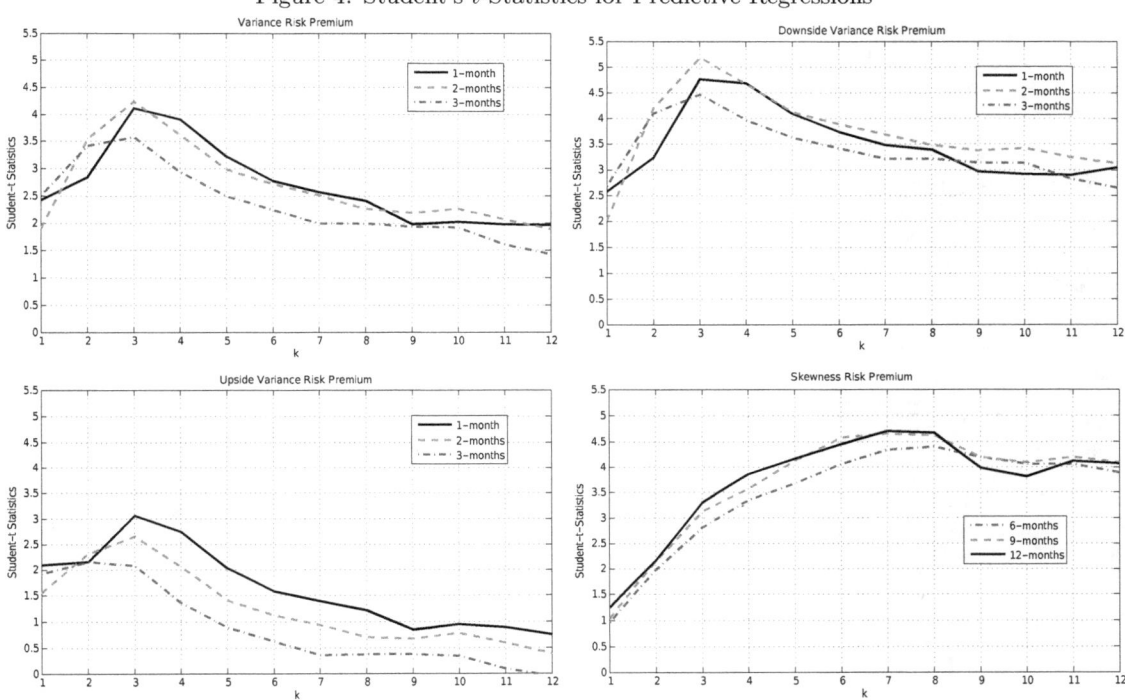

These figures plot the t-statistics for slope parameters of predictive regressions – Equation (12) – constructed following Hodrick (1992) from heteroscedasticity and serial correlation consistent standard errors that explicitly take account of the overlap in the regressions. The predictors here are variance risk, upside variance risk, downside variance risk, and skewness risk premia. In these figures, k is the prediction horizon, ranging between 1 and 12 months ahead. To simplify the figures, only three aggregation levels – h – are shown.

Figure 5: Adjusted R^2 for Predictive Regressions

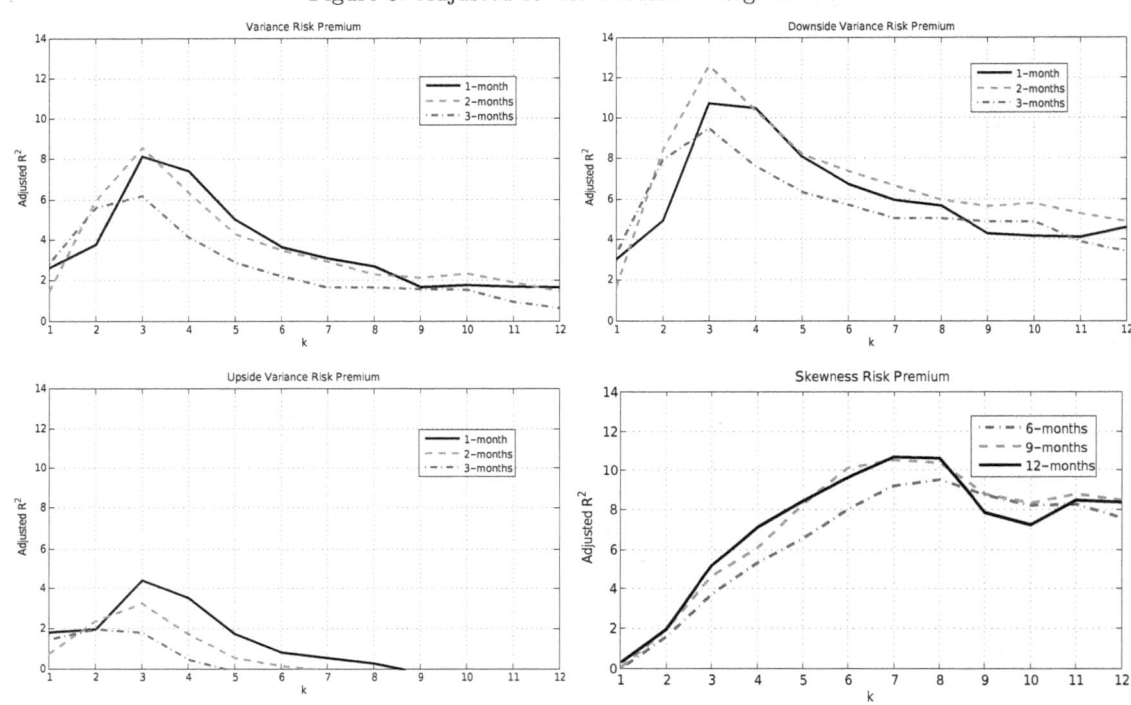

These figures plot the adjusted R^2s of predictive regressions – Equation (12). The predictors here are variance risk, upside variance risk, downside variance risk, and skewness risk premia. In these figures, k is the prediction horizon, ranging between 1 and 12 months ahead. To simplify the figures, only three aggregation levels – h – are shown.

Figure 6: Comparison of Adjusted R^2s for Risk-Neutral and Physical Variance Measures

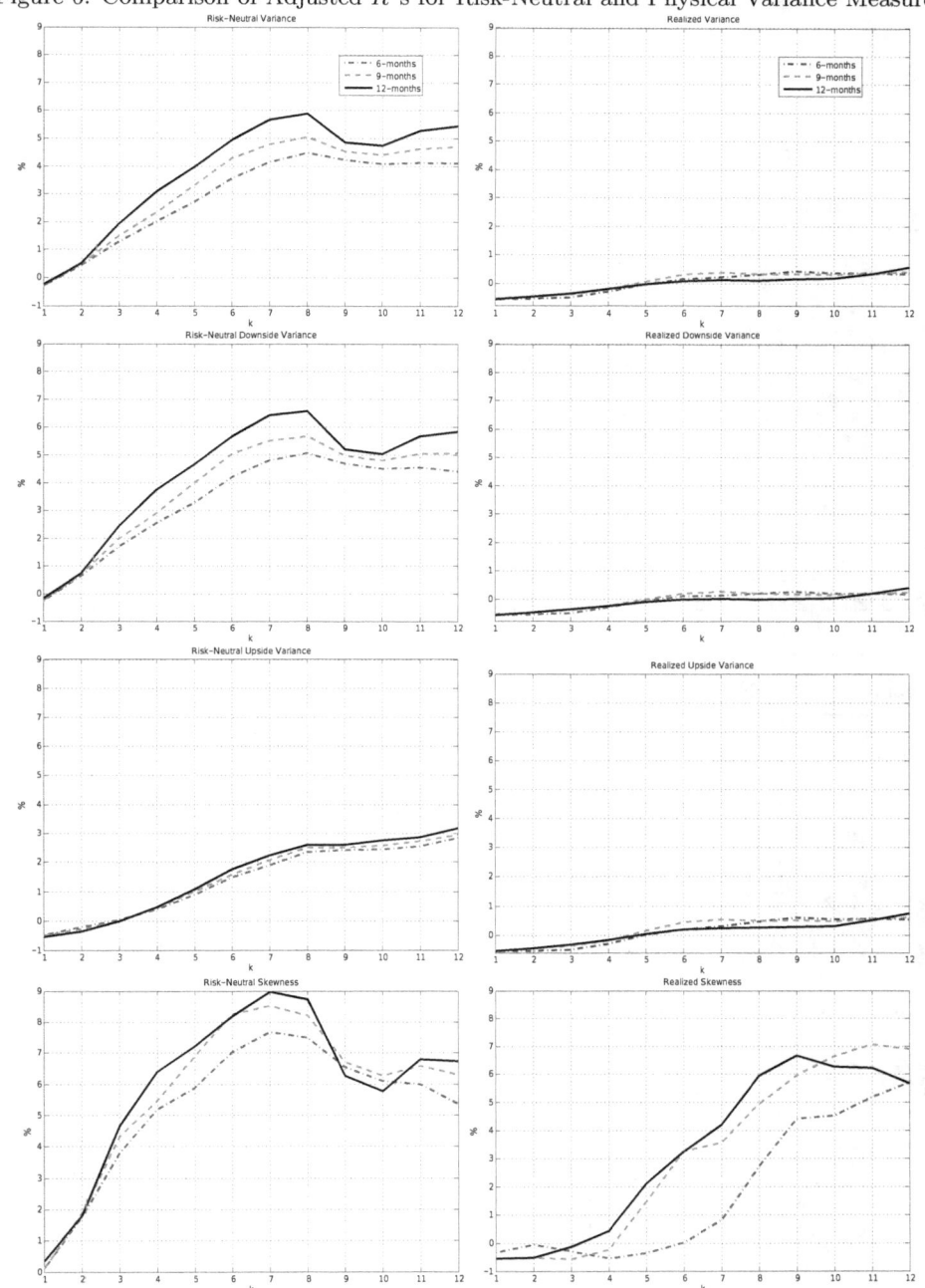

These figures plot the adjusted R^2s for predictive regressions – Equation (12). The predictors here are risk-neutral and realized variance, upside variance, downside variance, and skewness. In these figures, k is the prediction horizon, ranging between 1 and 12 months ahead. To simplify the figures, only three aggregation levels – h – are shown.

Figure 7: Time-Series for Variance and Skewness Risk Premia

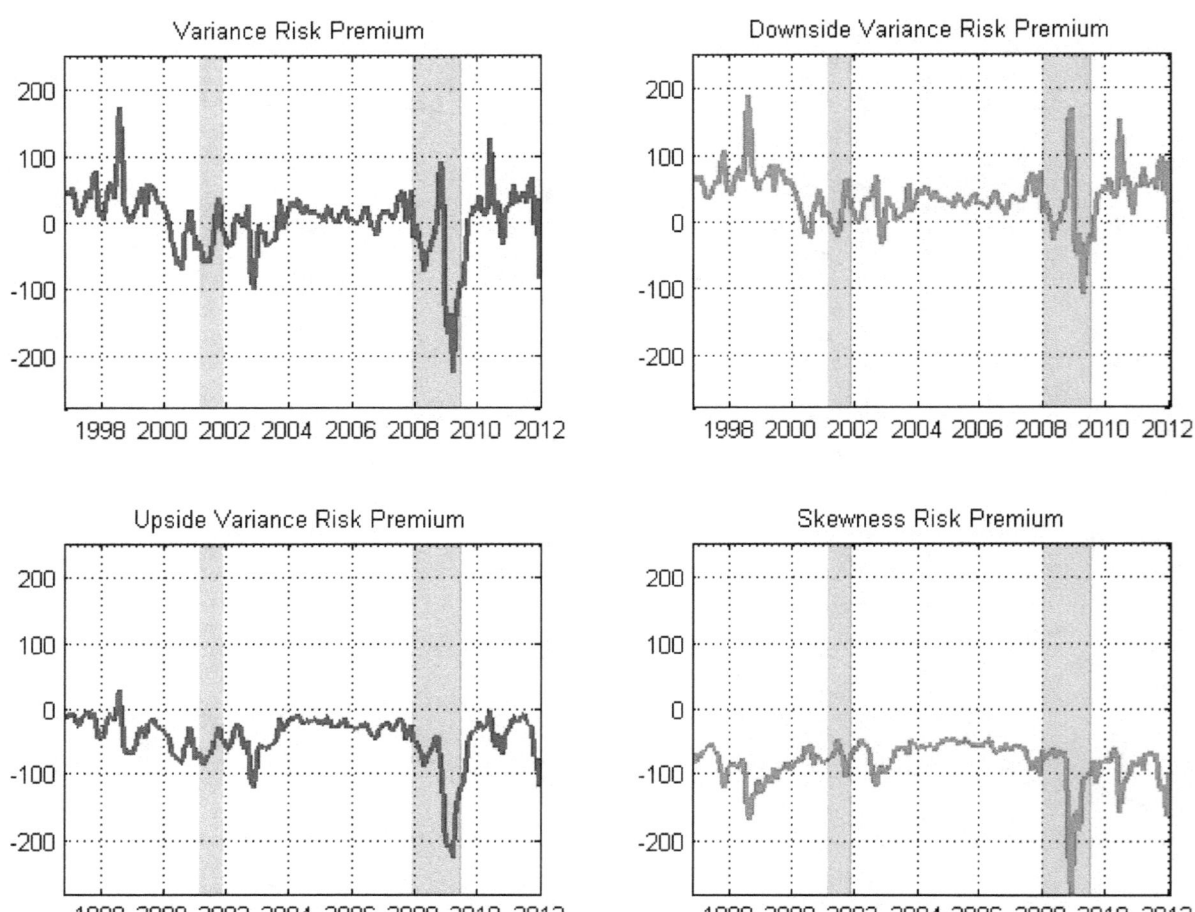

These figures plot the paths of annualized monthly values ($\times 10^3$) for the variance risk premium, upside variance risk premium, downside variance risk premium, and skewness risk premium, extracted from U.S. financial markets data for September 1996 to December 2011. The shaded areas represent NBER recessions.